THE HISTORY

OF

76 SIEGE BATTERY

R.G.A.

L. F. PENSTONE

The Naval & Military Press Ltd

published in association with

FIREPOWER
The Royal Artillery Museum
Woolwich

Published by
The Naval & Military Press Ltd
Unit 10 Ridgewood Industrial Park,
Uckfield, East Sussex,
TN22 5QE England
Tel: +44 (0) 1825 749494
Fax: +44 (0) 1825 765701
www.naval-military-press.com

in association with

FIREPOWER
The Royal Artillery Museum, Woolwich
www.firepower.org.uk

*In reprinting in facsimile from the original, any imperfections are inevitably reproduced
and the quality may fall short of modern type and cartographic standards.*

Printed and bound by Antony Rowe Ltd, Eastbourne

FOREWORD

The following chapters have been written for three reasons.

Firstly, to illustrate the activities of 76 Siege Battery R.G.A., from its formation until the end of the Great War.

Secondly, to record the wonderful spirit of comradeship and good fellowship that existed amongst the officers and men at all times.

Lastly, in the present day, to keep fresh in our minds the sacred memory of our comrades who fell in the War.

CONTENTS

INTRODUCTION

It is appropriate that mention should be made of the circumstances under which this History came to be written.

The first Reunion Dinner of former members of 76 Siege Battery R.G.A. was principally due to the efforts made by Major F. A. W. Cobbold, D.S.O., and Q.M. Sergeant A. E. Potter, and, presided over by its first Battery Commander, Major R. H. Brent Clark, took place on 27th March, 1926.

During that evening, L. F. Penstone suggested that an Old Comrades' Association should be formed, and that under its auspices a dinner should be held annually. His proposal was unanimously agreed to, and he was asked to submit a plan, to be adopted as soon as possible, for the formation of such an Association.

At a specially convened Meeting held prior to the Annual Dinner on the 26th March, 1927, a Committee was formed, Rules adopted, and the Old Comrades' Association, on which the A.S.C. (M.T.) Column was represented, came into being.

Since that date the Dinner has been held annually, with an average attendance of about 60.

On these occasions, quite apart from the interest provided by the speeches and the excellent entertainment of the artists, there is the added pleasure of meeting old friends and being able to talk over the times we spent together, training in England and afterwards in France. These annual gatherings mean a lot to those who attend them, and if possible grow more popular every year.

Now for the History. The idea was Penstone's, and he has done the greater portion of the work. There follows a list of those who have made contributions to it, but the fact remains that without him it would never have been written.

The first stage, which was that of extracting data from

7

THE HISTORY OF 76 SIEGE BATTERY R.G.A.

War Office Records, commenced at least nine years ago, and it is on this foundation that the main story has been built, supplemented, of course, by contributions from those who kept diaries or, alternatively, were in a position to add something to the bare skeleton we had to deal with. It has seemed at times as though the work would never end. Certain it is that without the zeal and determination which Penstone brought to his task, the job would have been abandoned long ago. He deserves, and will receive, the congratulations and thanks of us all.

The thanks of all members of the Old Comrades' Association are due to the following for contributions, loans of diaries, assistance in checking the text, examinations of proofs, etc., etc.

Major R. H. BRENT CLARK.
Major F. A. W. COBBOLD, D.S.O.
Captain F. H. ASHWORTH.
Lieutenant P. B. SHOWAN.
A. BENTALL, M.M.
J. K. BIGSBY.
D. E. ROSE, M.M.
M. TURNER.
W. H. LOWREY.
J. E. PERCIVAL.
W. LOCK.
H. THOMAS.
J. A. WATSON.
H. E. PALMER.
F. ABBOTT.
J. PAPWORTH.

F. H. A.

THE HISTORY OF
76 SIEGE BATTERY R.G.A.

CHAPTER 1.

FORMATION AND EARLY TRAINING.

The history of No. 76 Siege Battery is to a large extent bound up with that of the Essex and Suffolk R.G.A. Half the personnel of Officers and men were drawn from this unit; the Battery was formed at Harwich; and the Commanding Officer, Major R. H. Brent Clark, had acted as Adjutant to the Essex and Suffolk R.G.A. (T.) for a considerable period prior to the War. From September, 1916, until July, 1917, the Battery was commanded by Major F. A. W. Cobbold, D.S.O., an Essex and Suffolk Territorial Officer, and in November, 1918, there were still present in the battery Battery Sergeant-Major A. E. Potter and fifteen members of the original party.

The other half of the Battery, drawn from the Regular Army, Special Reserve and Kitchener's Army, came from all parts of the country; whereas the Essex and Suffolk half were drawn from a comparatively small area, and not unnaturally exercised an influence such as might be expected from a body of men brought up with the same local traditions.

It was in August, 1915, the news arrived that Harwich had been chosen as a depôt for the formation of Siege Batteries, and that Major (afterwards Colonel) G. W. Horsfield, O.B.E., the Commander of No. 1 Company Essex and Suffolk R.G.A., had been chosen to undertake this work. The territorials were posted to Beacon Hill fort at Harwich under the Command of Captain F. A. W. Cobbold, who had as his junior officers Lieut. F. H. Ashworth, of Harwich, and Lieut. A. Sandercock, of Southend.

At Beacon Hill there was little or no material with which to drill, so improvisations were the order of the day. The officers had previously undergone courses of instruction at Lydd, but when they were drafted to batteries, the absence of guns and the almost total lack of equipment of any sort or kind proved a severe handicap, and it was with the greatest difficulty that they were able to devise programmes which would fill up the day. Naturally route marches and physical training bulked very largely in the programme. Signalling courses came next, but the utmost ingenuity had to be exercised in gun training (there being no guns) and in courses of instruction on dial sights, etc. Old lumber and any sort of equipment took the place of guns, but as one or two expert carpenters were members of the Battery, very creditable productions in the way of imitation directors and dial sights were soon forthcoming.

As 76 Siege Battery was the first battery in which half the strength was to be formed from the Essex and Suffolks, it was a great day for Harwich when this half of the Battery, composed of drafts from Harwich, Felixstowe, Southend and Stratford, marched down to Harwich Station, preceded by the band of the Essex Regiment, and followed by every available Officer and man who could be spared from duty, and Lieut. Ashworth's Cairn terrier, Datum, a favourite with all the Battery. The route was lined by friends and relatives, and everybody was in high spirits, and felt that for them at any rate the War had at last begun. The destination was Horsham, where the Essex and Suffolk half joined up with the remaining half composed of Regulars, Special Reserves and Kitchener's men, making one unit under the command of Major Clark, with Lieut. E. N. Aston and Lieut. E. Starkey as his two other Subalterns.

During the time the territorial half were in training at Harwich, Capt. R. H. Brent Clark, who had in the meantime been promoted Major, was as a result of this promotion given the command of 67 Siege Battery.

Having been previously connected with Harwich, and with the knowledge of the constitution of one half of 76 Siege Battery, Major Clark—having had something to do with the arrangements beforehand whilst adjutant—put in an application to take command of 76 instead of 67, and after an interview with General Hickman this was granted.

He then proceeded to Clarence Barracks, Portsmouth, to choose his men for the other half.

On the parade ground were lined up about three hundred men—regulars returned from France invalided but again fit, and recruits of the new army, and from these majors of newly-formed batteries were selecting their men.

An interesting and unusual experience for both selectors and selected not without its amusing side. Specialists were in demand, and the usual question was : "Have you any qualifications." One man answered "None, sir," but Major Clark, thinking him a likely choice, asked his name. "NUNN, sir," he replied. "I know; I didn't ask your qualifications this time—just your name." "NUNN, sir," was again the answer. A bit impatient this time the Major asked, "Can't you tell me your name— N.A.M.E." "NUNN, sir, N.U.N.N.," and that is how he joined the battery.

With the union of the two sections a period of some two or three weeks was spent at Roffey Camp, Horsham, where the battery used 8 inch and 6.6 muzzle-loading howitzers for drill purposes.

As some of the men specially selected by Major Brent Clark at Portsmouth had already experienced some months active service in France with siege batteries, they greatly helped in getting the battery efficient and effective within a comparatively short space of time.

In December the Battery moved to Lydd, where it passed its shooting tests very creditably. Here the Battery had its first experience on modern 6 inch guns, 12 inch howitzers on railway mounting, and equipment such as was used in the field, though the actual firing was carried out from 8 inch muzzle-loading howitzers—the charge being black powder, and the range table based on practice carried out in 1879. Muzzle-loading drill had to be learnt specially to fire these guns. Drill was also carried out on the 9.45 Skoda howitzers used in the South African War—but all the ammunition for these had been used before the turn of the Battery came to fire.

Warnings of hostile aircraft were fairly frequent, and one night at about 10.30 p.m., in response to one of these, the whole of the battery was turned out on to the parade ground.

For a while everyone listened intently for the drone of aeroplanes or zeppelins, but nothing could be heard, and with the period of patience passing, whispering and the the shuffling of feet began to break the silence. The officer in charge of the parade, keen to hear if any aircraft was about, mildly raised his voice more in appeal than command, "Keep quiet, keep quiet, did anyone hear anything?" A slight lull in the noise, but the whispering of those wishing to be back in the huts, etc., started again, followed by that appealing voice, "Keep quiet, keep quiet, did anyone hear anything?" It being of no avail, the parade was dismissed, after a time which seemed hours. Next morning the left section did their shoot, and just after the first gun had fired with a h—— of a bang, Gunner Quigley's voice was heard in the same appealing tone, "Did anyone hear anything?"

The period at Lydd lasted some four months, being prolonged by the long wait for equipment. At a later stage in the War, when the ammunition question had been solved, batteries came in, did their firing practice and went out in a fortnight, but at one time it seemed to us at Lydd as if the War Office had forgotten all about us, and only the fact that the batteries who were there before us moved off to France at irregular intervals, served to dispel this illusion. Lydd is a cold, bleak, windswept spot, and from the "Leave" point of view, by reason of its isolation and distance from the places whence the officers and men had been drawn, was most inconvenient. Nevertheless it had its compensations. Folkestone and Hastings were not far distant, and afforded attractions of a welcome character.

At all events we continued our training, with route marches and occasional "field days" near Appledore, on which occasions the signallers laid out lines from "O.P's" to battery, and the observers took the opportunity of doing some ranging, with the help of "puff" parties who fired small smoke bombs some distance away. There was also night digging, and one evening the right section were paraded to prepare a firing position in readiness for practice the next day.

The night turned out rather badly as far as the weather was concerned, so a call to the left section for assistance was sent out. Somebody evidently "got the wire," as a small party, including a corporal and a few gunners of the left section, managed to secrete themselves under the table in the library at "Tin Town." Whoever was responsible for the idea was certainly a genius, for that ill-lit hut was seldom used. Even the orderly sergeant failed to find them when he examined the room.

The chief merit of Lydd was the extreme sociability of the units assembled there. It was there that we met 69 Battery, of whom half was composed of Sussex R.G.A. Territorials, 67 Battery with half of its personnel North Scottish R.G.A. Territorials from Dundee, and the five South African Batteries, 71 to 75, between all of whom and ourselves the most satisfactory and friendly relations existed.

These relations were cemented later on when we found ourselves in France, because, as luck would have it, we were all drafted to pretty much the same sectors.

However, everything comes to an end, and about the 15th of March the majority of the Battery left Lydd to mobilize at Bristol. Parties were detailed to pick up stores at Woolwich, and in due time they and the main body met at the White City, Bristol, which was our final camping ground in England. Here we were joined by three officers and about 70 N.C.O.s and men of the A.S.C., who formed our transport column. Our equipment consisted of four 9.2 howitzers with the usual stores—4 caterpillar tractors, 34 Commer lorries, including one workshop lorry, 2 Vauxhall motor cars and service motor cycles.

For a few days parades were comparatively easy, and on March 24th guns, stores and lorries were prepared for shipment *via* Avonmouth.

Chapter II.

THE SOMME, MAY, 1916-JUNE, 1917.

On March 27th an advance party, under Lieut. Aston, left Bristol for Southampton, embarking on the commandeered L.S.W. Rly. "Hantonia" at 7 a.m. on the 28th for Le Havre, which was reached after a severe crossing in a gale at 3 p.m.

After a day's rest at No. 4 Rest Camp at the docks, the party entrained for Rouen, where the day was spent until 4 p.m., when the party left for Abbeville. From here, by short stages through Doullens, Puchevillers, and Bouzincourt, the party arrived at Albert, where strangely enough it was billeted at "76" Rue d'Amiens on April 2nd.

Without delay the advance party set to work on a position in the rear of the railway cutting west of Albert, at a point flanking both sides of Hennencourt-Albert road, with the Albert-Amiens road on the extreme right. During the next few weeks, while awaiting the arrival of the main body of the battery, guns and stores, the advance party made dug-outs and prepared the gun emplacements.

The main body of the Battery left Bristol on the 31st March and embarked at Southampton for Boulogne on the S.S. "Lydia," together with 69 Siege Battery, commanded by Major H. G. Carr, in whose Brigade the Battery were afterwards to serve. 69 Battery had trained with us at Lydd, and we met them several times later in the War. On the voyage, the "Lydia" kept close to the English coast and sailed without lights. We arrived at Boulogne at 1 a.m. on the morning of April 1st—"All Fools' Day" —disembarked at 7.30 a.m., and marched up to St. Martin's Camp, where we stayed for just over a fortnight, awaiting the arrival of guns, ammunition column, etc. Whilst at St. Martin's Camp, time was spent in fatigues at the docks, medical and kit inspections and a few route marches. Everyone was impatient for the arrival of the guns and stores, and these arrived on the 14th April on the S.S. "Crown of Aragon," which had been delayed a fortnight owing to a report of hostile submarines in the Bristol Channel. It is a matter of interest that a sister ship to the "Crown of Aragon" was torpedoed and sunk off Boulogne within a day or two of the latter's arrival with the equipment.

When the guns eventually arrived, fatigue parties were marched to the docks to assist in the unloading. While the work proceeded the party experienced the first air raid since arriving in France. Two days later the guns were entrained at the quayside under an escort, and on the 17th April the Battery left St. Martin's Camp in lorries for Talmas, halting at Ruisseauville and Doullens on the way.

The Battery remained at Talmas for nearly a fortnight, during which time the guns arrived and the first mail from England was delivered. Here for the first time the battery was practised in drill and in mounting and dismounting our own guns and platforms. Most of the members of the Battery had only seen 9.2 howitzers in pieces "en route," and it was a great advantage to have these few days at Talmas in which to learn how to lay the firing beams and mount and dismount the guns. Fortunately there were a few men in the Battery who had been in 10, 12 and 13 Siege Batteries (some of the earliest to be equipped with 9.2s), whose practical experience was invaluable to the other members of the battery.

Much friendly rivalry took place between the four sections over the speed in which the gun emplacements could be made, baulks laid and the guns mounted for action, and so proficient did they become that eventually only about one-third of the time specified in the drill book was taken to carry out this work.

Such keenness and zeal brought about fine results, and as subsequent events proved, the gun teams of 76 were always able to overcome their tasks, however difficult. A set of four excellent gun teams.

On the 21st April a further detachment was sent to join the advance party in Albert, and when paraded by the Battery sergeant-major were informed by him, "You men, you're going up the line and you *ain't* coming back!" This was not taken literally, of course, and caused much amusement.

The positions allotted to the left section were in two dummy haystacks on the left side of the Albert-Hennencourt road. These dummies had been previously occupied by guns of another battery, whose line of fire was more to the right than ours, and at night time it was necessary to lift the dummy stacks and turn them more to the left in order that they would fit in with the centre of the line of fire. These "haystacks" occasioned a good deal of swearing among the men at times, as it was necessary to patch them up after each shoot, and the remark, "We are supposed to be gunners, not ruddy farmers," was often heard. The right section were in gunpits, dug out of a bank on the right-hand side of the Albert-Hennencourt road. Cutting into this bank, getting through the chalk seam, the safe disposal of the white chalk, and the consequent making of wire netting camouflage to screen the white pits from the air, caused a vast amount of work.

By May 11th everything was ready, with the guns mounted and ready for registration.

The last of the Battery left Talmas on the 1st May and most of the personnel were accommodated either in tents, dug-outs or huts at the battery position, and only a few were in billets at Lavieville. During the fine weather about this time, frequent bathing parades were held in the river Ancre, across the main road from Albert to Amiens.

The Battery was assigned to 25 H.A.G., commanded by Lt.-Col. C. W. Clark, and we became 10th Corps troops, under the command of Brig.-Gen. H. O. Vincent of the 10th Corps heavies. The position allotted to us, however, was in 3rd Corps area, and as the batteries on each side of us were 3rd Corps troops, we were often visited by Brig.-Gen. T. N. Perkins, commanding 3rd

Corps Heavy Artillery, when he was visiting his other batteries in the neighbourhood. With his assistance we were able to draw much material in the way of pit props, corrugated iron, etc., from the 3rd Corps stores, in addition to a similar amount which we drew, as of right, from the 10th Corps, so that we were able to build extra good dug-outs and huts.

The officers and B.C. staff having ascertained that the centre of our line of fire was approximately Thiepval, spent some time looking for O.P.'s, but found that nearly every suitable position had been labelled "Reserved for 27 S.B." Certain observation posts were allotted to us, numbered 325, 326, 327 and 333, and the signallers were engaged in laying lines direct to Group Headquarters and to the above-mentioned observation posts. The construction of O.P. 325 fell to the lot of a working party from the Battery under Lieut. Starkey one wretched wet night. The O.P. took the form of a hollow splinter-proof box open at the bottom and half of the back with a slot in the front. This was then camouflaged with plaster of Paris to represent earth and placed in line with the rest of the parapet in a narrow communication trench close to "Jacob's Ladder" north of Mesnil. The trench was afterwards christened "Bathside Avenue" as a reminder of Harwich.

Incidentally, this trip at night was the first near approach to the line that any member of the Battery had made, and the journey through the semi-ruined village of Mesnil, with the eerie glare of star shells and the occasional whistling of snipers' bullets, gave the party an insight into what war really meant.

The other O.P.'s were already built and lines of communication laid, including the line to 25 H.A.G. Headquarters at Bouzincourt, from which exchange we could be put into communication with 10th Corps Headquarters.

The first shoot was observed from O.P. 333, and a corner in the enemy trench in front of Thiepval was selected as the point on which to register the guns. As this was on the reverse slope from the O.P. extremely good observation could be obtained. The observation party consisted of Major Brent Clark, Capt. Cobbold and a small party of observers and signallers, who had their first experience of being definitely under fire, for they were greeted with a few whizzbangs. The shoot was carried out satisfactorily, and by this time the work in the battery position, including dug-outs and construction of cover, had been completed. Shooting regularly took place and many points in the enemy's lines were registered.

About this time an additional officer, Second Lieut. R. W. Satchwell, was posted to us, and he remained with the Battery until he was killed in action on the 31st January, 1917. A French interpreter was also posted to us, and Staff-Sergeant Bottomley, from Vickers works, came to assist in keeping the guns in order and look out for any defects so they could be avoided in any subsequent marks.

It soon became evident that a big engagement would take place in the near future, as large numbers of troops were always on the move and more batteries came into position. Our immediate neighbours were 26 Siege Battery with 6 inch guns, and 69 Siege Battery with 9.2 howitzers, on our left flank, whilst on our right was 48 Siege Battery, which had only recently arrived from Egypt, and manned 8 inch howitzers. Across the Amiens road was a R.M.A. battery with 15 inch howitzers, whilst in front of us were many 4.7 gun batteries, 4.5 howitzers and eighteen-pounder brigades.

After the 19th May many targets were registered and several of these were shelled regularly by the Battery, which even at this early stage in its career was shooting in a very satisfactory manner.

One effect of our position being in 3rd Corps area, which was to the right of 10th Corps area, was that we were almost always firing to the left of the centre line of the guns. In course of time this caused all the guns to assume a tilt, and two or three firing beams were broken whilst the Battery was in this position.

Life in the Battery went with a swing, each man pulling

his weight. Occasional trips into Albert, Bouzincourt, Lavieville and other nearby villages—where there were cafés—coupled with occasional games of football and cards —bridge for the officers, pontoon and nap for the men— together with the mail from home, all helped to keep up the spirit of the battery, which soon seemed to grow into a big family of good comrades.

Firing took place daily, and apart from trench targets the Battery had the satisfaction of quietening enemy trench mortars. On June 5th the battery took part in an hour's bombardment of enemy trenches at Thiepval from 11 p.m. to midnight, when the Border Regiment raided the enemy trenches and took 100 prisoners. The Battery expended 100 rounds on this occasion.

A quiet spell for the Battery ensued for some days, and time was occupied largely in making accommodation for and receiving heavy supplies of ammunition, and constructing a forward gun position in Authuille Wood to which to move if the offensive was successful. (This position, however, was never used, as we were required to hold our old position for a long time after the offensive began.)

From 24th June a general increase in firing took place along the sector, and daily our guns were active, shelling strong points in Thiepval, notably the Château, machine-gun emplacements, and Mouquet Farm, an enemy stronghold which later on proved a great obstacle to our infantry. Enemy batteries became more active and responded. Albert was often shelled heavily in return for our fire, and many attempts were made to bring down a R.F.C. kite balloon somewhat in our rear. As we were almost in line, we very nearly got some of the bad shots, which fell at just a comfortable distance from our "A" gun. Hostile aircraft also became more active, and almost every day air fights took place above our heads.

During the evening of the 25th June, together with our flank batteries, 61, 48, 26 and 69, we began a slow bombardment. Firing continued at an increased rate from 4 a.m. on the 26th, and during the day we expended 520 rounds, and it was noticed on this day that further south the firing became much heavier, which seemed to predict " something doing."

From 27th June the bombardment increased in intensity and our guns were tested to capacity, and one day "A" and "B" guns fired 130 rounds each between midnight and noon, and "C" and "D" guns 125 each between 6 a.m. and noon, in spite of vigorous protests from our Staff-Sergt. Bottomley, A.O.C., who exclaimed bitterly, "You are not equipped with machine-guns." It was certainly asking rather a lot for a 9.2 howitzer, a gun that was made to stand only about 6 rounds per hour.

Originally it had been intended that the attack should take place on the 28th June, but the weather was so bad that it was put off day after day, until finally zero hour was fixed for 7.30 a.m. on July 1st.

During the period from the 28th to the 30th June inclusive we were continually in action, and could see large numbers of troops in lorries and on foot proceeding towards the front line, and many field ambulances going forward. These, with the ammunition columns of both heavy and field artillery, not only filled the roads, but created an animated and most impressive scene, and the cheerful spirit of all concerned seemed to bode well for the result of the attack.

Throughout the night of 30th June desultory firing took place along the line, and judging by the continual flares and Verey Lights in the sky, there was an alertness in the front line trenches.

The morning of July 1st broke fine and warm, and the gun crews were on their posts at an early hour, standing by till at 6.30 a.m. the allied bombardment opened intensively. The 10th Corps, commanded by General Morland, which the Battery was supporting, consisted of the 36th, 49th and 32nd Divisions, was placed between the 8th Corps on the left and the 3rd Corps on the right, and had as objectives the German positions in the neighbourhood of Thiepval.

We were engaged on enemy trenches and strong points in and near to Thiepval and our bombardment lasted till 10 a.m. Zero hour for the infantry was at 7.30 a.m. and success was immediate: objectives were gained and held along the front upon which the attack was launched, chiefly to the south, except at Thiepval, a very strong point of the enemy, where stout resistance was met and our infantry had to fall back with heavy loss.

As the day wore on we were confronted with much of the toll of war in the shape of the continual stream of ambulances, and men slightly wounded, slowly making their way back to dressing stations. Though there seemed to us a great number of these, it was but a small proportion of the casualties, apart from killed, that the British Army sustained that day. We were consoled, however, by the reports received of successes, and these soon had a telling effect on all concerned, as great importance was attached to this Somme offensive, and we knew that at last we had got the enemy on the move.

At 9 a.m., however, we discovered that the Germans were not to be so easily driven back, for they set up a counter-attack which opened with a heavy bombardment, to which 76 and all batteries replied. In spite of these counter-attacks little or no ground was given, however. About noon Major Clark, accompanied by a signaller, "Dan" Rose, went forward, with the object of finding a new site in Thiepval, but had to return disappointed, as it was still held by the enemy.

Towards the evening things quietened down a little, and the "breather" came as a welcome to the gun teams who had worked hard and exceedingly well. The following day was quieter, and we were cheered to receive a report from H.Q. commending the Battery on its good shooting.

The attack was continued throughout the following days, and much progress was made in the South, but 76 were still engaged in bombarding the neighbourhood of Thiepval, which still held up the advance and seemed likely to do so for a considerable time.

The fine spell of weather suddenly broke and heavy thunderstorms with much rain made conditions bad for a few days, and to some extent had an adverse effect on operations.

So far the Battery had been happily blessed with good health and no casualties, and everybody kept up with wonderfully good spirit, but the luck did not hold too long. Lieut. Ashworth was the first to be put out of action, being caught in a barrage on his way to the O.P. on July 5th. Happily his wounds were not serious, and after being taken to a dressing station he was able to return to the Battery the same evening, only to be evacuated to the base four days later on account of the bad shaking up he had received.

The only part of the German line in our immediate sector, which was captured and held on the 1st July, was a corner of the "Leipzig Salient," and targets were allotted to 76 and other batteries extremely close to this small corner, which, a few days after the 1st July, was being held by the 1st Wilts. Regiment, commanded by Col. S. S. Ogilvie. Complaints were made that some heavy shells from British guns had fallen in this small area, and one day a target was allotted to us in the German front line, just to the right of the small Sector held by the 1st Wilts. The 1st Wilts were nervous that our shells might fall in their sector, so Capt. Cobbold was ordered to report to Col. Ogilvie; firing was not to commence until he got into communication with the Battery and reported that every available man was under cover. When Capt. Cobbold pointed out on the map the target which the Battery had been ordered to engage, Col. Ogilvie particularly asked that it should not be attacked as a mine had been laid practically under the spot. However, it was found impossible to get in communication with the Battery as the telephone line had been damaged by shell firing, and as the 1st Wilts were shortly afterwards going "over the top," Capt. Cobbold returned to the Battery and no firing took place on the allotted target.

There was no evidence that any shells from 76 had fallen amongst the 1st Wilts, but shells from some British siege battery were believed to have done so. So far as is known 76 was never accused of firing into our own trenches, but as will appear later on in this history, we had to refuse to shoot with one gun which was so worn that we could not rely on its accuracy, though the amount it was worn was not sufficient to enable the ordnance officers to condemn it.

In spite of the bad weather and mud the attack was continued, and we got busy again on the morning of July 7th, when enemy positions were shelled until the afternoon, and another further success was gained on the right flank. By now several batteries had moved up with the advance, and although we had reconnoitred and examined a few new positions, we still remained on at our position, where it looked as though we would stay until Thiepval—our main target—was taken.

With all this continuous firing our guns stood the test well, but on July 7th however the rifling of "A" gun was blown out by a premature in the bore and it had to be dismantled and sent away. Happily this caused no casualties in the Battery, though the gun crew were laid flat. A large piece of the shell landed in the position of 36 Siege in Albert, but fortunately did no damage. 69 Siege, on our left, was not so fortunate, as a few weeks earlier they had a premature just outside the muzzle, which caused several casualties. However, in spite of the heavy test, our guns had so far stood, the shooting had been very satisfactory, and much credit was due to the Battery and especially to the B.C. staff.

The weather now began to improve, and on July 9th we fired at targets in Thiepval and Ovillers la Boiselle, and as the firing lasted from 11 a.m. till 8.30 p.m. at the rate of five rounds per hour, it was a long, gruelling day for the gunners. Happily the weather was fine and warm, and they were able to discard all clothes except trousers and boots, a delightful concession under the circumstances.

Daily bathing still continued in the Ancre, where again minor swimming contests took place, for at the spot where we bathed the current was very strong, and some seemed to delight in trying to beat the current. The bathe was usually followed by the general "de-louse" and for a time —usually very short—everybody felt clean, refreshed and comfortable.

During the next few days activity continued, and when we had the pleasure of witnessing the 1st and 2nd Life Guards riding up for action, it appeared as though a break was going to be made.

About this time the 10th Corps were taken out of the line, and 25 H.A.G. was transferred to the 2nd Corps Heavies, under the command of Brig.-Gen. Logan. The 2nd Corps was in the reserve Army, which later became the 5th Army, having been transferred from the 4th Army about this time.

For a short while we ceased to fire at targets close to Thiepval, and engaged targets more to the right, and this necessitated the use of one or two improvised O.P's in part of what had been the German lines before the 1st July. The bombardment was concentrated chiefly on Pozieres and Contalmaison, leading up to an attack on these places. On the morning of July 11th, however, when the former was attacked, our infantry suffered heavy loss and no advance was made. A little further south, at Contalmaison, it was reported that the cavalry had gone into action. The day finished with a success again to the south, and reports stated that 9,000 prisoners had been taken to date.

We continued to lose our neighbours, who were moving forward, 69 and 48 Batteries both leaving us about this time, and 76 was slowly but surely being isolated. For many days we continued in action, during which time we pegged away at our various targets, especially Pozieres, which was holding up the advance.

"A" section got their new gun and Major Clark received the following despatch from H.Q. : "10 a.m. 16.7.16. All goes well on British Front. 2,000 prisoners captured during past 24 hours including Reg. O.C. 3rd Prussian Guards Division. Total prisoners on British Front exceed 10,000" AAA. The following was also received, "Army Bulletin 11 a.m. 16/7/16 AAA. We have captured all of Delville, Bazentin-le, Petit Woods and part of High Wood, and hold line of main road between those woods. Attack on Pozieres did not succeed but we hold the line Z4 C23 X 10 a 45, X10b 88 AAA. Some hundreds of Germans captured, also five 8" howitzers, three 5.9 howitzers, four 5" siege guns, four field guns, and three other howitzers. Six German aeroplanes destroyed in last 24 hours, including three Fokkers and one double-engined machine AAA."

These despatches were received with enthusiasm, and we felt that our efforts had contributed towards the successes gained. The attack on Pozieres was unsuccessful, but on July 19th the Australians passed our position, and it was following a determined attack by them that the village fell into British hands. It was a well fortified spot, but following daily bombardments for about a week, the Aussies stormed and passed through Pozieres on 25th July. During this period of the attack on Pozieres—July 19th being the day—Lt. Sandercock and Cpl. Wringe both had fortunate escapes from hostile fire, a shell landing close to them. Both were badly shaken, and Lieut. Sandercock was evacuated to hospital with shell shock.

Albert was now a daily target for the enemy, and often occasional "spares" came near to the Battery position when the Amiens road was under fire. Fortunately, however, we still kept comparatively free from casualties.

The push in towards the south of Thiepval opened up fresh spots for observation purposes, and an advance O.P. was occupied by our observers, and it proved to be in a warm corner, amongst support and communication trenches, in what was left of the village of Ovillers-la-Boiselle.

Presumably to await further plans, the Battery shooting quietened down somewhat, but an evening bombardment, in which many batteries took part, constituted a fairly regular item in our orders. This bombardment was mainly concentrated fire, and must have caused a hot time for the enemy gathered at the spot selected, which was usually a village.

The last few days of July passed off in fine hot weather, and it was noticed that enemy aircraft were increasing in numbers and becoming more active, and a warning to this effect was issued by H.Q.

August broke fine; enemy aircraft were still very busy, and on the 2nd the German artillery began to shell heavily, from 11 a.m. to 12.30 p.m. This same day we bombarded the enemy's second main defence north of Pozieres and his front line. These two points occupied our attention for the rest of the day.

We continued to get through a large amount of shooting and the gun teams were hard put to it, but stuck it extremely well. Day and night alike we still kept busy, though the night stunts were less strenuous. The Boche airmen were still active, flying in relays and at times low, and we began to fear that our position would be discovered. Extra care was taken, especially with regard to "C" and "D" guns in their respective "hay-stacks" to conceal the position. It appeared, however, that the Boche machines were chiefly engaged in registering their batteries on prominent points in Albert, chiefly the railway station, bridges, billets and the Amiens road. Included in his "hate" were a few lachrymatory gas shells, some of which fell close to the left section guns on the evening of August 6th. Heavy firing continued on both sides, and air fights became fairly frequent, but on the 8th the German guns quietened down a bit, and following a hard day's shooting it began to rain. With changed conditions for a couple of days 76 eased up a bit.

On the morning of the 11th a heavy fog produced an uncanny calm and in consequence a temporary truce, which did not last long, for when the fog cleared we opened fire strongly and heavily. Our guns worked overtime, and during one spell, an hour at mid-day, 200 rounds were dispatched, and by 8 p.m. 440 rounds had been expended. Later the same evening "D" gun fired 85 rounds in a period of 52 minutes, surely a cruel infliction on a 9.2 howitzer. Staff-Sergt. Bottomley would have collapsed, but unfortunately the gun did not, though it had to be cooled down with wet sandbags. The targets at this period were Mouquet Farm and strong points and trenches close to Thiepval, which was still proving a formidable obstacle. At this rate of firing it is not to be wondered that our supplies of ammunition became short, and, in fact, occasions did arise when shells were taken straight from lorry to gun and fired.

On August 14th we disposed of 600 rounds, and the lorries came up from railhead dumps five times during the day, some even going up towards "the line," to other batteries, to bring back ammunition to us. This entailed a great deal of hard work unloading, cleaning shells and firing, and the gunners were hard put to it.

This intense firing led up to another attack on the 18th, when once again our infantry were successful, being well supported by artillery, as the following reports received will prove. To O.C. 76 S.B. : "I wish to congratulate the heavy artillery on their excellent work to-day. We have gained our objective, and about 400 prisoners" AAA. From 2nd Corp H.A., 18/8/16. Copy received 19/8/16 from Army Commander, Reserve Army : "Please congratulate all troops who took part in yesterday's attack on the excellent performance AAA. I was able to see the attack of the 145th Brigade AAA. The way in which they advanced into our barrage was beyond praise, and it reaped its reward AAA. The artillery co-operation was also excellent, and reflects great credit on all concerned AAA. Please accept my best congratulations for yourself and all concerned AAA. Repeated for information" AAA. From 25th H.A.G.

On the day of this success our column was evidently

spotted on its arrival with shells, and confirmation came with a bracket on "D" gun, but only a few rounds were dropped near. Our next bit of excitement was on August 21st, when a flight of enemy planes came over. Two of them flying low over the battery dropped six bombs which fell to the rear of us. The worst we had to endure was the flying shrapnel and splinters from our own A.A. guns, but though pieces were flying about the vicinity of the battery nobody was hit.

We were very cheered and pleased to receive the following "pat on the back." "Aug. 20th. Corps Commander, 25th H.A.G. Express appreciation of work done by 76 Siege Battery during operations. Thanks for support. Not only was the shooting of the Battery excellent, but conduct of men worthy of the traditions of the R.A."

Till the end of the month the Battery fired each day, and the men had plenty of work to do unloading and cleaning ammunition, as heavy rains had made much mud. The "haystacks" too had to undergo repairs, as they were beginning to get slowly blown away by concussion. The weather became patchy and a heavy thunderstorm broke on the 29th whilst the Battery was in action. This caused a deal of trouble, for as our position was in a slight valley we were soon under flood conditions. The following day much energy was needed in cleaning up the shells in readiness for the next day, when 400 rounds were fired on Thiepval. After this "D" gun broke her baulks, and had to be dismounted, and two days later "C" gun did the same thing. Within four days, however, the Battery had full gun power, and once again got busy with Thiepval as the target.

The German guns renewed their shelling of Albert and the roads leading in and and out, and an ammunition dump to our left came in for heavy "strafeing." Artillery was active on both sides, and as the German guns became more active we were not surprised when the enemy counter-attacked during the night of September 7th. Chlorine and tear gas shells arrived, necessitating a gas "alarm," but the effect was short-lived. We joined in the reply during the night and continued until daylight, when we ceased fire.

About this time the Boche planes began to drop propaganda from the air urging the French to revolt against the British, who, they said, "would never leave French soil otherwise," and referring to the "English" channel ports of Calais, Boulogne and Le Havre.

A mild scare was occasioned one day when an S.O.S. came through. Suspicion fell on a farmer who worked the slope in front of "A" and "B" guns, so Lieut. Sandercock, Gunners Bentall, Last and Bigsby approached him, and in their best text-book French tried to make him clear out of the district. But all to no avail, until Quigley, coming up, exclaimed, "Hi, ... off." Then he vanished like smoke.

During the few months in which we had occupied the position the country surrounding the Battery had slowly undergone a vast change. What had once been fields, even cultivated, were now practically roads or paths, muddy patches and, in many places, not a sign of the green we first saw. Digging and transport too made a difference, and with huts and dug-outs, ammunition trenches, telephone poles and lines, the ugly effect of war and its spoliation were now more pronounced. It may be added here that close to the guns we had dug shallow trenches in which the shells were deposited and covered with camouflage. Later these were filled in and the shells placed near the guns, where they were kept free from dirt.

At the rear of the right section the Royal Engineers had just erected a large field trough for horses. It was constructed of stout canvas, being about twenty feet square and three feet deep, held above ground by stout posts. Columns of horses from adjacent R.F.A. and transport lines came there each day and this caused much dampness and mud, and recent heavy rains made conditions very bad. It was not long before this trough was spotted by Boche observers when on their daily aerial reconnoitring, and on September 8th, about mid-day, when a troop of men brought their horses to water, they were greeted by a sharp burst from a German 5.9 gun battery. It created considerable confusion, and a stampede which at one time looked dangerous, but the drivers with great courage handled their mounts well, and though a few casualties were caused amongst men and horses, the excitement soon passed off. One shell fell only ten yards from "B" gun, but no casualties occurred amongst our men.

On the 8th September Major Brent Clark left the Battery, being admitted to hospital suffering from a breakdown, and Capt. Cobbold took command, and about this time Second Lieut. H. V. Irwine was posted to the Battery, and we also had Lieuts. Stringer and Browne added to our strength.

By the 9th September the bombardment was still continuing, and in the afternoon we fired 100 rounds, and though the pace slowed down we continued firing during the night. In the morning the left section were ordered to advance, and the guns were dismounted and moved forward to some distance east of Albert, on the north side close to the Albert-Baupaume road in the neighbourhood of Usna Hill. In this position we had as neighbours slightly in our rear 8 Siege Battery with 6 inch Mark VII guns, under the command of Capt. C. P. G. Cameron (who was later killed in action). The blast of these guns was very trying and nearly demolished the Armstrong hut which served as the Officers' Mess.

Nearby were the dug-outs and horse lines of a heavy battery which one day became the objective of a hostile battery. Some shells fell fairly close to our guns without harm to any of our men ; some, in fact, took advantage of the bombardment to scrounge amongst the horse lines which had been temporarily evacuated. Corporal S—— and Gunner Q—— found the canteen and in it a nine-gallon cask of real beer, which was promptly "won" and hidden in the precincts of 76 Siege Battery, but where? Corporal W—— with Gunners R—— and D—— did their best to find out, and were holding a "Council of War" when Lieut. Satchwell appeared, leaving an officer of the "Heavies" who lost the beer some thirty yards away.

Lieut. Satchwell : "Corporal W——, a cask of beer has been stolen ; this officer is looking for it ; do you know where it is?"

Corporal W—— : "No, sir, it is not in this half of the battery."

Lieut. Satchwell (*sotto voce*) : "It damned well is, because I saw the cheeky devils bring it over here."

Corporal W—— (also quietly) : "Well, sir, we have looked all over the place for it, but have had no luck."

Lieut. Satchwell (to other officer) : "You can come and have a look in these dug-outs, old man, but this corporal assures me that they have not seen it, and I am damned sure if beer had been in this battery these blighters would have found it."

The Heavy officer departed satisfied, but the "blighters" were not until they at last found it and, unknown to the two scroungers (Cpl. S—— and Gunner Q——), filled every mess tin and water-bottle they could get hold of.

After we had been here two or three days, some peculiar objects arrived, and were the subject of much conjecture and interest, as no one knew what they were, and we could get no information about them. They were heavily camouflaged, but by dint of enquiries we ascertained that they were the first consignment of what afterwards became known as tanks, and they made their first attack from this position.

Both sections of the Battery were engaged on different targets, the right section being still in its original position, having its main line of fire in the neighbourhood of Thiepval, whilst the left section was attacking Mouquet Farm, Schwaben Redoubt and other strong points. Slowly these points were captured by our troops, Mouquet Farm only after very severe fighting. The position at Usna Hill was not nearly so comfortable as our original position as there was much more shelling in the neighbourhood and a considerable amount of heavy shrapnel bursting overhead. The left section were really assisting in the preparation for the attack of September 15th, which was on a wide front to the south of Thiepval, and in this the tanks were first used. The villages of Courcelette, Martinpuich and Flers were captured, and the success was partially due to the surprise caused by the tanks.

When, following a heavy bombardment, Thiepval was finally captured, the line was considerably straightened. Ever since the Battery had been in action it had been more or less continually bombarding Thiepval, and not until this was captured was it possible for the right section to move forward. This section was far in the rear of most batteries in the neighbourhood, having been kept specially for the purpose of bombarding Thiepval. Shortly after this both sections were re-united, as on October 1st the Battery took over three guns and their position from 13 Siege Battery at Ovillers la Boiselle, we still retaining "D" section's original gun.

Our new position was totally different from the one we had left, the guns being mounted close to what was the original German front line before July 1st. Some of their very spacious dug-outs made excellent accommodation for the majority of us, and odd huts and splinter-proof shelters were occupied by the remainder. The Officers still retained the Armstrong hut for the mess. The country here was pitted with many shell holes, whilst close by and slightly to the rear was the crater of La Boiselle, a reminder of July 1st. La Boiselle, on the Baupaume road, was on our right, but we were closer to Ovillers on our left. Both these villages were in ruins, but proved useful for "scrounging" purposes, especially as now there was a nip in the air and fuel was needed for the stoves that Jerry had left behind—one thing for which we had to thank him.

Conditions were now not so comfortable as Albert was was well behind us. Our one consolation was a small Y.M.C.A. canteen hut on the Baupaume road, but the occupier held no licence—"on or off"— and so we became more or less teetotal (the mess excluded). The only "kick" the gunners got was the rum issue, which was always most welcome; working conditions, too, were harder, but this was only to be expected. Signallers and observers had roads to take longer and rougher and also more hazardous, our O. Pips being now either in disused trenches or at the old château at Mesnil, a derelict mansion, and a pet target for Jerry.

About this time the method of procedure adopted was for all batteries in the neighbourhood to concentrate on different villages occupied by the enemy for a short period at a different time each day, and we concentrated on Grandcourt, Pys, Miraumont, Irles and other villages somewhere behind the German front line.

The weather was gradually becoming more wintry and we were not called upon to fire quite so much, though there were periods when we had to undertake considerable bombardments, and we had a certain amount of night firing. Up to October 21st "D" gun, the only one of our original guns still remaining with us, had fired 6,000 rounds, the highest number per day being recorded as 399 on September 26th (by November 14th this gun had fired 7,200 rounds).

For a time when in this position we were engaged on counter battery work, and on October 25th four hostile batteries were engaged in response to N.F. calls, the result being satisfactory, a direct hit being recorded on one enemy gun. These shoots were, of course, carried out with aerial observations, and the observer in one case told one of the officers that our first round was an O.K. on the target. The fact that the Battery was so well registered as to be able to do this reflects great credit on the B.C. staff, especially on Bombardier Bentall, who worked out a new muzzle velocity for each gun every evening on the result of the observations of the day's shooting. The importance of this is more evident when it is explained that when the Battery first came to France we were only supplied with

shells with the old gas check type of driving band and
cordite as a propellant, but after a while a shell with a hump
driving band was issued and we were supplied with new
cartridges. These were sent up indiscriminately, and it
was never known what type would arrive next; consequently a muzzle velocity for each gun with each combination of shell and propellant had to be worked out.

Correspondence took place between the R.A. authorities in France and those in England, and it was pointed out
that from experience in the field, that especially in worn
guns, the muzzle velocity when the hump type of driving
band was used was less than when the gas check type was
used. The authorities in England informed the authorities
in France that experiments had been carried out on Salisbury Plain, the result of which demonstrated that there
was no difference in the two types of driving band; but
our experience was different, and after the issue of the
hump type we always found a different muzzle velocity
from each gun with the two different types of driving band.

On November 3rd, through the assistance of Col.
C. W. Clark, an exchange of officers took place, Lieut. S.
Godlee, who had been with the Essex & Suffolk R.G.A. at
Landguard, being transferred from 36 Siege Battery in
exchange for Lieut. Stringer.

The ground in this position was pitted with shell holes,
and considerable difficulty was experienced in getting the
ammunition to the Battery, which was about 300 yards
off the main road at Ovillers. A Decauville track was laid,
which owing to the shell holes took a winding course, and
was very often out of action owing to the softness of the
ground, as many truck-loads of ammunition came off the
track through the spreading of the rails. Oddly enough that
well-known song "There's a long, long trail a-winding"
was just popular, and it certainly made a good theme song.
The ammunition practically always arrived at night, and
it was very hard work in the dark putting the trucks on the
rails after they had been readjusted, and re-loading them
with ammunition covered with mud. This task in such

wretched conditions was undoubtedly one of the worst the men had to stand up to, and not too much can be written about it. It must have been hellish, and self-control surely played a great part, relieved only by an outburst—and many a "flow of language" accompanied the "ammo" on its shaky way down the Decauville track to the guns.

During one of these nightly duties of unloading, a very amusing incident occurred, although Gunner Looker thought otherwise. At the start of the Decauville track a platform had been erected on to which to roll the shells from the lorries before they were man-handled on to the bogey trucks. At one end of this platform was a deep shell hole or "sump" about ten feet square and four feet deep, full of liquid mud of the consistency of pea-soup. Here stood Gunner Looker on the platform with his inseparable pal "Bingo" Ling, waiting for the lorry to back up to the platform with the last few shells to complete the right half-section's quota. Left half-section was waiting to carry on, and it was raining.

Gunner Looker : "Come on, driver, get your ruddy lorry back; we're in a hurry and don't want to get wet to the ruddy skin !"

The driver tries, but the lorry wheels skid in the mud of the road.

Gunner Looker : "Go forrard and then shove her back. Give her some juice and step on it, mate !"

Driver does so, hits the platform with a bang; Looker sails into the air off the platform and down over head into the "sump" and eventually appeared on the surface like a sea lion at the Zoo, covered with slimy mud. Having scraped some off with his hands, he burst forth with a torrent of abuse and " ?" language. "Drivers yer call yerselves ? —— drivers yer ——, yer couldn't drive a —— nail !"

Gunner Ling : "What's up, Sammy ? Did yer fall or was yer pushed ? Come on, mate, let's go to see if the quarter-bloke has a pair of pyjamas for yer to sleep in to-night."

We were engaged in preparing for the attack

on the 13th and 14th November, when the Royal Naval Division successfully stormed Beaumont-Hamel and Beaucourt, and 76, assisted by aerial observation, succeeded in destroying several enemy strong points. During this operation we were given as a target two very important enemy support trenches known as "A" and "B" near Beaumont-Hamel. They were right out of our area, but someone at Corps H.Q. had a brain-wave and discovered that 76 could enfilade them. We could just engage them by switching to our extreme left. Capt. Aston observed the shoot, and after we had ranged and had a good long spell of battery fire he reported, "These trenches are completely destroyed." This was confirmed by an O.C. of another battery, believed to be Major Carr of 69, who was in the O.P., and he was much impressed by the result.

The following message was received on November 15th from C in C to Sir Hubert Gough : "Re results of operations on the 13th and 14th when the R.N. Division attacked with success. Accuracy and rapidity of fire was excellent."

Officers, observers and signallers will remember the very spacious dug-out at Hamel which, as a result of this attack, was at our disposal, and what a wonderful piece of mining work it was.

A party of 76 signallers were operating with other signallers from the R.N. Division and a Scottish Division during the capture of "Y Ravine," Beaumont-Hamel. They were laying telephone lines in the fog with Lieut. Satchwell in command and reached the above-mentioned dug-out so recently vacated by the enemy. It must have been about one hundred feet deep and about half-a-mile long, with outside entrances at intervals of fifty to one hundred yards.

Besides the sleeping quarters, mess rooms and kitchens, there was quite a nice officers' lounge, and above all, an operating theatre and a well-equipped dressing station.

The following day certain of the Battery officers made a tour of inspection with one of the signallers as guide. Airing his knowledge gained the previous day he showed them round, and came to a church bell which had been installed for some reason by the Germans, and was now being used as an alarm by a battalion of our infantry who had occupied the dug-out. In ignorance of the present use of the bell the guide, still eagerly airing his knowledge, rang it. This created a beautiful row and trouble for "Dan" Rose, the guide.

Here the Boche certainly left behind something very substantial and useful, as part of it was eventually used by us as a tapping-in station when an O.P. was made nearby.

The weather set in rather cold and wet, and the N.C.O.s and men were thankful for the goatskin issue. Various minor operations helped to straighten out the line, our targets being chiefly on the Boche front and second lines and surrounding villages in their occupation on the north side of the River Ancre. Early in December the weather became very cold, with keen heavy frosts, which though a bit trying, made conditions easier for transport, and lightened the task of dumping shells along our little Decauville track.

Shortly before Christmas Battery S/M. Chinnery left the Battery on being due for discharge, and we understood would have nothing further to do with the war. However, he immediately re-engaged, and was seen by some of the members of the battery later. His place was taken by Battery S/M. A. Martin, who had seen much service, and remained with the battery for a long period. About this time, towards the end of December, Lieut. P. B. Showan was posted to the Battery, *vice* A/Capt. E. N. Aston, transferred.

Various other moves had been made amongst the N.C.O.s. Bombardiers O. Mallows and J. Grundy left to take up commissions, Sergt. G. Potter posted to another battery during November, Q.M.S. "Pony" Moore to a base school as instructor in siege gunnery, and Sergt. F. Streeter to 27th Siege Battery during December. Later on Bombardier E. Shee, followed by Corporal J. Watson, also left for commissions, so from time to time we lost the services of some valued N.C.O.s.

On Christmas day, though there was no truce, very little gun firing was undertaken, and all in the Battery did their best to enjoy themselves under the circumstances. Some time before, a pig christened "Dennis" had been purchased, and this was kept in the Battery and fattened for Christmas, and when killed by Gunner Durrant made excellent Christmas fare.

After Christmas the weather became very cold indeed, the thermometer falling below zero many nights, and it was difficult to keep warm. Fuel was very scarce, and many quarter charges from the cartridges were burned, along with such damp wood as could be gathered. One day the Battery was in great luck, as the driver of a lorry which had been sent to the Ordnance Depôt to get a spare part for one of the guns, on his way back saw several lorries queueing up near a coal dump, so he joined in the queue and came back with a load of coal. Orders were issued against damaging dug-outs for the purpose of obtaining fuel, but damage was often done. Even so, by some means or another, fuel was obtained, as the little chimneys of the dug-outs continued to carry off the smoke of good fires. With the severe frost there also came a scarcity of water, but although fortunately a supply was found a little in front of our position at Spring Gardens, this did not always satisfy the needs, and men often went out with cartridge boxes to collect snow and ice in order to make tea.

In the first few weeks of 1917 we were kept busy, and several new enemy trenches appeared in front of the Schwaben Redoubt, which was used by us as an observation post. We were supplied with maps and aerial photographs of these, and had to attack them as soon as they appeared. In particular, we engaged new trenches known as "Rum, Tea and Coffee trenches."

On the 31st January, 1917, Lieut. R. W. Satchwell was killed in action in the Schwaben Redoubt. One of the party of signallers with him, an eye-witness, gives the account as follows : "The early frosty morning was bright and sunny. Whilst waiting for the haze to lift, Lieut. Satchwell stood chatting to some observers of another battery. With the morning sun behind them they evidently stood out as a target, seeing that the O.P. was on the sky-line, and the Boche gunners were quick to realize it. A bracket and two other shells close by were followed by the fatal shell, which dropped in the trench and exploded within a yard of the dug-out entrance where we three signallers were seated. The concussion knocked us down the dug-out stairs, but recovering and going outside, we found that Lieut. Satchwell had been badly hit in several places. He was killed instantly." His body was taken back to the Battery and laid to rest in the little cemetery at Ovillers, a cross being erected to mark the grave of one whose death came as a great blow to the Battery in general, as he was an excellent officer and popular with all ranks.

Early in February, owing to further advances, we received orders to move towards Pozieres to a position on the right of the road just above Spring Gardens. The move was a very difficult one as the temperature was below zero and the earth in the earth boxes, which had been sodden with rain water, was frozen solid, and it was impossible to take the boxes to pieces. After burning much petrol on the outside of the earth boxes, however, the contents were sufficiently thawed to dismount them. Great difficulty was experienced in starting such of the lorries as would start at all, and many of them were kept running all night, to avoid the necessity of having to start them up again when they were required. Lieut. S. Godlee was at this time (12/2/17) promoted Acting-Captain, and Lieut. S. Hann was posted to the Battery.

Shortly after we took up the new position, the thaw set in, and we were engaged in firing on German front line trenches. It was in this position that it was noticed that one of the guns was firing very erratically. Lieut. Starkey, in the observation post, observed an O.K. with one round and the next round fired at the same elevation fell quite close to our own front line, which was at this place about 1,000 yards from our target. The O.C. refused to use this gun any more, and it was examined by Ordnance officers, who, after taking sundry measurements, reported that the gun was not sufficiently worn to condemn, but we did not use it for some time, and the O.C. got it condemned in the next position.

As the enemy had retired a considerable distance, the Battery was ordered to take up a position at Martinpuich on March 3rd, and soon two guns were mounted by the side of the road there. The other two guns had at last been condemned, and as yet had not been replaced. Whilst in Martinpuich we were working in closer co-operation with the infantry than formerly, and a telephone line was laid to the front line and a liaison officer appointed, and signallers completely equipped were told off for liaison purposes. However, almost at once the enemy retired a long distance over a considerable front, leaving many traps and much polluted water, etc., and so for several days after the retirement there was nothing for the Battery to do.

The Vauxhall car, driven by Private Wright, had been sent to the A.S.C. workshop for repair, and it was replaced by a very dilapidated Wolseley with a strange driver. In this car some of the officers went to Baupaume, and had only left a short time when the Town Hall was blown up by a delayed-action mine left by the enemy.

The night before the Battery was ordered to move, Major Cobbold went to the A.S.C. H.Q. to see whether the repairs to the Vauxhall car had been completed, and found that the car had been ready for several days before, and that the O.C. of the A.S.C. had appropriated our Battery car and its driver Private Wright. Private Wright was found in his billet and fetched the car and returned to the Battery without seeing the O.C. of the A.S.C., leaving the dilapidated Wolseley behind.

This retirement of the enemy brought to a conclusion

the Battle of the Somme, and within a few days we received instructions to pack up and move to the Arras front. The following conversation between two signallers before the move may be of significant interest.

1st Sig. : "Thank goodness we're leaving. I'm fed up with this —— front, and it's time we had a shift !"

2nd Sig. : "Don't you be too keen on a shift ; we've been fairly cushy here, and there are worse places than this. You wait and see."

(It may be added the 1st signaller (H. W. Jones) was killed in action four months later at Ypres.)

We said good-bye to 25 H.A.G., in which we had been ever since our arrival in France, with very much regret. Our relations with Col. Clark and the other officers had always been very happy, and we had received great kindness and attention from the Medical Officer, Capt. Lyon. He visited us practically daily, and very frequently lunched in the Officers' Mess. He kept our Battery Medical Orderly, Pte. Wilson ("Count Iodine"), well equipped and very efficient. Our ammunition at Martinpuich was in a deplorable state, many of the shells being buried in mud, and though we were ordered to move "with full echelons," it was found impossible to take any of the ammunition with us.

The number of lorries available for this move was so small that kits and bedding had to be reduced to a minimum and, most tragic of all, a large quantity of new clothing, etc., in the Quarter Master's store, for which the men had been clamouring for weeks, had to be left behind. A place was found, however, for the cook's dog, which had been run over by a lorry, but which by careful attention survived the injury.

The authorities were anxious to have a grand parade of the batteries moving off from this area to the Arras area, and this was arranged to take place in the Square at Albert, but as most of the batteries were very anxious to get on the move, only a small contingent went to the parade.

During all our stay in the Somme area we were very

well served by our ammunition column, which usually brought large quantities of ammunition at suitable times, from a military point of view, though the men usually had to turn out to receive it when they least wished to do any work. The officers of the ammunition column changed from time to time, but all the officers in the Battery will have grateful recollections of an A.S.C. Subaltern, named Buckeley, who was familiarly known as "Uncle Sydney," and who often invited them to the A.S.C. H.Q., which were infinitely pleasanter and more comfortable than ours.

Chapter III.

VIMY AND ARRAS.

The trek to our new sector commenced in the late afternoon of March 9th, and at places lorries had to be manhandled through the muddy roads, but Herissart was eventually reached at night, and billets were hurriedly found for all. The next night was spent at Doullens, and from there the Battery travelled through back areas and undamaged countryside to a new position at Maroeuil, which was practically undamaged. In one of the villages on the journey, Mr. Showan became very popular amongst the men, as he managed to find a field cashier and pay was issued, which was very acceptable.

We were pleased to find that we were detailed for 13 H.A.G. (1st Army Canadian Corps) commanded by Lieut.-Col. H. G. Carr, whom we had known when he was in command of 69 Siege Battery. The position allotted to us was in a small wood in which four concrete emplacements had been previously prepared, situated slightly in front of Maroeuil, with the ground falling away to the Arras-St. Eloi road, which road was screened with Hessian; and warnings were posted up for the benefit of drivers, who were warned not to raise dust, on account of the road being visible from the ridge. When we started mounting the guns in this position it was found impossible to get the firing beams into the places provided for them in the concrete emplacements, and considerable delay was caused owing to our having to chip the concrete away all round to allow the firing beams to fit. On putting a gun to the test it was found that after the first few rounds had been fired the back firing beam broke up the concrete and the whole gun and mounting slipped back from the original position. Altogether we found the concrete "floors" quite useless, so fresh emplacements were dug.

In getting into this position at night one of the caterpillars broke down when the gun was on the open ground in front of the position and in full view of Vimy Ridge, and it was only just before daylight that we were able to man-handle it under cover, out of view. Our ammunition was brought up at night and unloaded from lorries at a point in front of us on the Arras-St. Eloi road, and from there a Decauville railway had to be laid at night to carry the ammunition to the battery. One day a flotilla of tanks "walked" over the track, destroying a long stretch, and our work in getting the ammunition to the battery was considerably hampered.

Two slight minor casualties occurred here, Gunners Coote and Lewis being wounded by the back-fire of T tubes.

This position was in full view of Vimy Ridge, and when elevated, the muzzles of the guns were well above the bushes. It was possible to stand a few yards from the guns and see the enemy trenches on the forward slope of Vimy Ridge, and we could also observe our own firing on these trenches from the Battery position. The group Commander realized that it was a dangerous position, and that as soon as we fired we should probably be spotted by the enemy, so we were informed that the only firing we should do before the attack on Vimy Ridge came off would be to register, and arrangements would be made for us to do this when many other batteries were firing, so that it would be less likely that we should be spotted. However, after registration, we fired daily, but fortunately were not spotted by the enemy.

There was a very large ammunition dump about three or four hundred yards to our right rear, and one afternoon this was shelled by the enemy and practically all the ammunition destroyed, so that it seemed almost miraculous that we received no damage to speak of in our position.

We found the observation posts in this area very different from those in the Somme, the one we had to use chiefly being in the neighbourhood of Neuville St. Vaast in a trench, in which the mud was practically up to the observers' knees.

The targets which had to be registered were at Thelus, La Chaudiere, Vimy, Farbus and enemy trenches on the Ridge, and certain machine-gun emplacements, and we were also employed on counter battery work.

There were many batteries in our neighbourhood, and we found our old friends, 69 Siege Battery, in a position in front of us, but they were not in Col. Carr's group. 27 Siege Battery, now commanded by Capt. Villiers, in place of Major C. W. Swinton, who was commanding 50 H.A.G., was also quite close to us.

By the beginning of April there was a very large concentration in the area and much firing took place daily, in preparation for the great attack, on the Arras-Vimy front as far as Vimy Ridge, which was to be launched on Easter Monday, April 9th. On the afternoon of Easter Sunday, the Battery was given an easy and enjoyable task, as our instructions were to fire 100 rounds into the village of Thelus, and do as much damage as possible. Very good observation was obtained from an improvised O.P. close to 69 Siege Battery's position, and it was seen that much bricks and mortar were dislodged in Thelus.

The attack commenced at 5.30 a.m. Easter Monday along the whole front, the top of Vimy Ridge being the objective of the Canadian Corps. Bombardment and barrage were very intense and spectacular, the whole countryside being lit up at about dawn. The artillery barrage worked perfectly, and the infantry had a much easier task than on the first day of the Somme. The Canadian Corps over-ran three lines of German trenches, including La Folie Farm, and captured the village of Farbus, and secured a total number of 70 officers and 3,500 men as prisoners.

During the afternoon of April 9th snow fell very heavily, and orders were received in the Battery to lay a wire up Vimy Ridge from one of the cores of a cable which had been laid to our front line before the battle. Our object was to be in a position to see and shoot on a certain trench just over the Ridge at 8 a.m. next day. Laying the cable over snowy ground across the trenches, which had only been captured that morning and where no clearing up had taken place, was a difficult job, but in the early hours of the morning the party arrived at the point which had been selected as the O.P., which was not far from the target which was to be engaged at 8 a.m. There seemed a number of our troops in the neighbourhood, and proceeding further, our party actually walked into the trench on which we had instructions to open fire, which was found to be full of our troops, who were shortly going to advance, as the enemy had retired during the night. Information was passed back to the Battery as the party found themselves only a few hundred yards back from a field artillery barrage in preparation for a further advance by the infantry.

The snowy weather which had temporarily set in made the work of the gun teams rather difficult. The gun-layers in particular were most handicapped as the heavy snow obliterated the objects used for laying, and the siege picket-lamps which in consequence had to be used were scarcely visible. The lamps quickly became covered with snow and the candles put out, so it was necessary to have gunners stationed by them to wipe off the snow and re-light the candles when necessary.

As the position immediately in front seemed uncertain, orders were received from the Battery for an O.P. to be found from which Petit-Vimy could be seen, and we were ordered to do as much damage as possible to that village with 100 rounds. The position was found rather to the right of the original point, and some of the most accurate shooting ever done by the Battery was observed. We had received two new guns, and 10 consecutive rounds fired at the same elevation were all observed to fall either in houses one side or other of a road in the village at right angles to the line of fire, or actually in the road itself. It is doubtful whether there were any enemy in Petit-Vimy at the time, as members of the Battery went there shortly afterwards and found the place had been very hastily evacuated.

For the next few days the Battery was kept busy, fire being concentrated on Avion, Oppy and the Hindenburg Line, and much successful shooting was done. On the 13th April the village of Petit-Vimy was evacuated by the enemy, who shelled it himself, and our own F.O.O., Lieut. P. B. Showan, went through Vimy and into Petit-Vimy later in the day.

Soon after, orders were received to move all our guns forward, and a suitable position was found in La Targette, so guns No. 2 and 4 were sent there with their detachments, under the command of Capt. Godlee. It was a not too healthy sort of spot, being situated to the left front of an important cross roads which was shelled heavily by a H.V. gun almost regularly every night. Severe casualties were sustained by the R.F.A. ammunition columns coming up with pack mules. Capt. Godlee did some fine rescue work on one particularly terrible occasion, when the road was littered with slaughtered men and mules.

The gun teams soon had the guns ready and in action again, firing on Avion and the railway near to it, as well as machine-gun emplacements and strategic points.

A few days later guns 1 and 3 were moved to a position in the ruined outskirts of Neuville St. Vaast. What was thought to be a very fine position with good solid foundations on which to place the firing beams, turned out very much otherwise, as when the lorry with the first set of firing beams backed into the position, one of the rear wheels crashed through the top of an old dead well, and it took some time after unloading it to get the wheels out and on to a firm platform of skidding, so we had to look for a more suitable position, which was found quite close. A considerable amount of firing was done by the two halves of the battery in these positions, but at the end of April we received orders for the whole of the Battery to move forward to a position south of Thelus on the Thelus-Rocincourt road. The position was actually on a road, with consequent easy registration for the Boche gunners, but we had the consolation of an ideal foundation for the guns, the sub-soil being chalk. Subsequent results of our good shooting can be traced in the first place to this fact.

The only possible way to get up the hill to Thelus was on a corduroy road of railway sleepers, and the position was very bare and exposed, except for one enormous German dug-out which would accommodate quite half of the Battery.

As soon as we arrived in this position at Thelus we were transferred from 13 H.A.G. to 76 H.A.G., a counter battery group under the command of Col. de Winton. We found that our immediate neighbour also on the right was 69 Siege Battery, with Major J. C. Lucas in command, and slightly on our right was a 12 inch battery commanded by Major Morris, whom many members of the Battery remembered as a subaltern in the early days of the War at Landguard.

We were daily engaged in counter battery work, and these shoots were chiefly carried out with aerial observation, though some were carried out from observation posts. From some of these some way in front of the Battery position, it was possible to get wonderful views of the back country, and on clear days the enemy could easily be seen in places which were quite beyond the range of our guns. There was continual fighting going on during this period, and as numbers of enemy guns had been captured, one or two siege batteries actually were able to get enemy guns into action, but we were not fortunate enough to get possession of one of these. Capt. Godlee may well remember a shoot from this position when he was playing a cat and mouse game with an enemy battery, and timing his fire in order to catch the German gunners in the open. They were doing their best to dodge our shells by firing and running, but we got an O.K. first.

The sequel, however, came about 7 p.m., when just as dinner was put on the table in the officers' mess a shell from the "destroyed" battery landed in front of No. 4 gun, to the discomfiture of four gunners playing cards round the loading platform !

This was followed by two "Ys" and a "Z" near the Armstrong hut forming the officers' mess, whereupon a well-timed sprint to the dug-outs was taken by the occupants—Lieut. Showan, with a leg of lamb (mutton) in one hand and a bottle of whisky in the other, beating most of the officers by a short leg and a full bottle !

One day we were visited by Lieut.-Col. H. St. G. Hamersley, who had been Gunnery Instructor at Landguard at the commencement of the War, and was then in command of a counter battery group, and whilst he was with us we were very heavily shelled by an enemy battery. Col. Hamersley seemed to know which battery it was, and gave orders to batteries in his group to open fire, and the shelling was stopped without much damage being done.

We were subjected to a considerable amount of shelling all the period we were in this position, and one day a number of the gun wheels of "69" were destroyed by shell fire, as they stood in the battery position preparatory to the guns being dismounted, and we had to lend "69" several wheels to enable them to get away.

Shortly after we had settled down here a railway was laid fairly near to our rear, and we were reminded of home when we saw a Great Eastern Railway engine arriving close to the Battery position.

On 17th May we were transferred to 50 H.A.G., with Col. C. W. Swinton, late of 27 Siege Battery, in command, and whilst under his command the Battery did some of the most effective counter battery shooting which it had done so far, especially in shoots with aerial observation, in which we were fortunate to have No. 57 Squadron R.A.F. as our observing squadron. The observer and the Battery Commander took a great deal of trouble to keep a personal contact between the Battery and the squadron. Major Cobbold, in fostering this understanding, generally talked to the observer on the telephone both before and after the shoot. Officers from the squadron visited and were entertained by the Battery on one or two occasions, and our Battery officers were also hospitably entertained on their visits to the Squadron, whose officers were of the best, especially one in whom we had the utmost confidence, an officer named Burlton, and with him as observer we carried out many successful shoots. Such success only came about by the smooth, complete co-operation of all concerned.

There is no doubt that the shooting of 76 at this period was excellent. The ranging of Major Cobbold, together with the precisely correct observations of the R.F.C. and our own visual observation officers, plus the élan of the gun teams, made a magnificent combination. 76 certainly won honours on this front, and we must have been an unholy terror to the enemy batteries which were selected as our targets.

One instance alone, an eye-witness account from the O.P., is sufficient confirmation of the deadly and destructive fire of 76 : "With the observation party at the excellent O.P. on the very crest of Vimy Ridge. Stretched out before us the broad plain of green fields, dotted here and there with pleasant little villages, whose red brick houses stood out clearly in the afternoon sunlight.

The target, as usual, a hostile battery, previously spotted by the R.F.C. and marked on the map, located in the S.W. corner of Mericourt, one of the little red brick villages, well out on the plain and to all appearance very little damaged—as yet !

The O.P. party had only a complementary job, as the R.F.C. observer was to range the battery. 'Stand by, plane now going up,' came the order.

In a very few minutes following the signal from the plane, 'No. 1 fired' is reported to the O.P. party, who remark, 'Here comes the first round.' We see a cloud of dirty-white smoke—very slightly short. Other bursts follow from the guns in turn, quickly bracketting the target —the old Battery seems pretty well on the spot right away.

Within a remarkably short space of time we hear from the B.C. post, 'All guns ranged—battery fire !' Then with fiendish precision 76 hurl round after round into that little corner of Mericourt. Thick clouds of red brick dust drift across the plain in the summer breeze. A fire is started, heavy clouds of black smoke mingle with the red, more fierce the fire from 76—'One, two, three, four !' Lieut. Showan is doing his stuff close behind the guns. A slight pause, and then again that merciless 'One, two, three, four !'

Huge columns of inky smoke shoot high in the air as exploding ammunition meets inevitable destruction. 'Plane reporting mostly O.K.' comes through to us from the battery. 'Good heavens, I should think so,' we reply. Then, 'We are going to do a little gun-fire,' and off they went. So with each gun crew now doing its damnedest, the bombardment redoubled in its fury, the target now becomes one seething mass of bursting shells and crashing houses. 'Mostly O.K.' from the plane,' they tell us from the B.C. post again—'He's going home, keep us on the target.'

We give an occasional slight correction, so little is required. Those gunners of 76 are like machines—inexorably they carry on till surely nothing can live in that little corner of Mericourt, which once housed an enemy battery, but is now nothing but a heap of smoking ruins, and the battery utterly destroyed. At last we give C.F.—76 has done it again !"

The following amusing discussion happened in the O.P. at the crest of Vimy Ridge. Capt. "Steve" Godlee is in charge of the usual little O.P. party, who seem slightly bored as there is very little doing at the moment. Suddenly one of the B.C. staff, no doubt imagining himself a budding B.C., says excitedly to the skipper : "I can see a Boche, sir !"

Steve (obviously bored) : "Well, what about it ?"

Budding B.C. : "There's a Boche battery marked there on the map, and that's one of the gunners walking about."

Steve (more bored) : "Well, what about it ?"

Budding B.C. : "Can't the battery have a go at him, sir ?"

Steve (with his best horn-rimmed glare) : "Certainly, if you, in your wisdom, can tell me what elevation the B.C. will give a 9.2 How. to engage a target 15,000 yards away."

Collapse of budding B.C., who suddenly remembers extreme range is about 11,500 yards.

We had several visits from Brig.-Gen. R. H. Massie, who commanded the Canadian Corps Heavies, and he was extremely pleased with the work of our gun detachments, and was especially complimentary about the extremely good timing of the salvoes which we fired. Many will remember the excellent way in which Mr. Showan timed the firing.

Shortly before we left Thelus a large ammunition dump in the village was destroyed by enemy gun firing, and a heavy battery, commanded by Major-Admiral Eyres, suffered severe casualties. Gradually the batteries round us were moved off, and on the 29th May we received orders to dismount the guns and move north.

When leaving his group, the Battery received a most complimentary testimonial from Col. Swinton, in the form of a message addressed to O.C. of the group to which the Battery was to be transferred, as follows :

To O.C. 70 Group,   "28.5.17.

Major F. A. W. Cobbold is leaving my group with his Battery 76 Siege to go north. I take this opportunity of expressing my appreciation of his excellent work.

76 Siege is about the best shooting battery it has been my good fortune to see, and it is in first class order. This is mainly due to Major Cobbold. I hope that when the time comes for honours and rewards, Major Cobbold and his Battery will not be forgotten.

(Signed) C. W. Swinton (Lieut.-Col.),
Cmdg. 50th H.A.G."

The journey to the north was very roundabout, as we proceeded *via* Arras, Bruay and through the marsh country to Hazebrouck, where we were rested for two days in a farm about a few hundred yards from the town. This was really the first complete rest the Battery had had since its arrival in France, and everyone enjoyed themselves in the town, in which were shops and cafés. The weather was fine, and the officers had an opportunity of visiting several interesting places in the neighbourhood, including Cassel.

It was very welcome, this short respite, and the rest was not interrupted at all except for three gunners—Bentall, Sawer and Hainsworth, who had taken advantage of the fine weather and were sleeping, sharing blankets, under a tree in the middle of a meadow. Some time about midnight one night came a growl from Sawer. "Hi, Bent, what the hell are you doing with my ruddy blankets?" Bentall : "I haven't got your blasted blankets!" Immediately a free fight commenced, which eventually embroiled Hainsworth. It only ended when they all discovered that one of the farmer's horses was strolling leisurely off in the moonlight with the cause of all the trouble in its mouth !

After a few days' rest here, the Battery left for Poperinghe, and having spent a night in billets, the final journey was made to our new battery position at Potton Farm, on the outskirts of Vlamertinghe. Incidentally, an advance party, with Corporal Western in charge, lost their way trying to find Potton Farm. They wandered well off their course, to be turned back by the military police—in the Square at Ypres !

CHAPTER IV.

YPRES AND THE SALIENT, JUNE, 1917.

The position we took was at a ruined farm known as Potton Farm, but shortly afterwards we obtained possession of Marsh's Farm, the rear part of which was still occupied by the farmer, and the members of the Battery made themselves as comfortable as possible in the outbuildings. We were now in 70 H.A.G., commanded by Col. Hardinge, and in the 8th Corps, the Artillery of which was commanded by Brig.-Gen. B. M. Bateman, with H.Q. in Vlamertinghe Château, and from whom Major Cobbold had a warm welcome, as he had been in command at Landguard for several years before the War.

As soon as the guns were in position we proceeded to register our targets in the neighbourhood of St. Julien. For this first shoot our observation post was a concrete pillar-box erected in the ruins of an old cottage, and much anxiety was felt as the first few rounds fired were not observed. At last, however, a burst was seen, and the F.O.O. and the B.C. were thankful to find that the lines of fire had been correctly laid out. The fact was, that we had been issued with some very well-painted, good-looking American shells, of which a very large proportion were duds, and it was not until after a special report had been sent that we got effective ammunition.

We were chiefly engaged on counter battery work in this position, and were subjected to a considerable amount of shelling, the enemy fire being chiefly directed on the roads. There was also a considerable amount of hostile shrapnel fire as a number of hostile kite balloons had good observation over the very flat country. The B.C. post, the most comfortable that we had since we arrived in France, was taken up in the cellar of Marsh's farm, and here Bombardier Bentall's B.C. staff were able to work under better conditions than ever before. The Battery, however, suffered several casualties, and the tasks of the signallers and observation parties were carried out under greater difficulties.

The gun teams, too, had their troubles, as owing to the marshy nature of the ground it was difficult to keep the guns on an even keel. A few rounds fired were sufficient to cause a list. Various means were tried to remedy this trouble, until it was found that the most efficient method was the placing of tree trunks under the baulks as extra foundations. (Before this could be given a fair trial, however, the order to move to "Wipers" was received.)

Aerial activity in the "Salient" seemed more intense compared with the other fronts we had visited, both by day and night, and during one night raid by a hostile machine a bomb was dropped close enough to cause one minor casualty, Gunner Hoffman being struck in the face by a fragment.

The work in which we were assisting was the preparation for the assault on the Messines-Wytschaete Ridge, and this took place on the 7th June, and was very successful. The famous mine which was exploded during this attack added to the success, and the shock of the explosion was felt in the Battery. The artillery support was very well carried out and assisted the infantry in maintaining the most important point once it had been taken. Our actual duties on the 7th June were of a stand-by nature. We had no definite target assigned to us, but were occupied the whole day in engaging targets which were allotted to us from H.Q. by telephone.

About this time the 8th Corps was taken out of the line and replaced by the 18th and 19th Corps, and we were transferred to the 90th H.A.G., under the command of Lieut.-Col. A. H. Thorp. This group was allotted to the 19th Corps, but our gun position was actually in 18th Corps area, and a large number of batteries found that they had been allotted to the opposite Corps to that in which their position was situated. At the time we were transferred to the 19th Corps we were also transferred from the 2nd Army to the 5th Army.

On the 21st June orders were received to prepare a position in the Cavalry Barracks at Ypres, and a party was sent to start the work, but soon after their arrival they were heavily shelled, fortunately without casualties, and although the progress of the work was rather interfered with, the day's task was eventually completed without mishap.

The following day the Battery was reinforced by Second Lieutenants Wallis and Butler, who with 32 N.C.O.s and men and two guns, made up our strength to a six gun Battery. Incidentally as several of the newcomers had been at Harwich and Landguard in the earlier days of the War, they were soon among friends. This detachment was part of a new Battery, 356, which brought out 9.2 mark 2 guns which, however, were handed over to 148 Siege Battery, a 4 gun Battery, and we took two of their 9.2 mark 1 guns in exchange.

With activity in the Ypres sector having so much increased, Poperinghe, and especially the station, was regularly shelled, and whilst waiting for the leave train, Sergt. Cornell and Corporal Western were wounded.

The preparation of the new position in the Cavalry Barracks took a considerable time, and although working parties were sent up daily, little progress could be made on account of hostile shelling. There were two ways from Vlamertinghe to Ypres, one via Belgian Battery Corner, the Gasworks, and round past the Infantry Barracks, the other, the main road past the Asylum, a hot spot! in which our working parties frequently took shelter amongst stacks of ammunition. This latter route was most often used, the party moving in single file with the officer in charge leading.

On the 24th June Capt. Godlee took a working party, including some new men who had reached the Battery only a few days before, to start work at a new position in the Cavalry Barracks. But the lorries could go no further than Kruiss Straat, where the road was being heavily shelled, and a halt had to be called. Shortly afterwards Major Cobbold arrived by car, and it was with the utmost difficulty that the men were able to get into the town. So it was decided that each man should go his own way over open ground, then over the bridge that spanned the canal, and find cover in sundry cellars, etc., but this spot had evidently been registered by the Boche to a nicety, and was one of his favourite targets. On this particular morning he was bumping it with 8 inch howitzers at intervals of about one minute, getting "O.K.s" on the pavé of the bridge with disconcerting frequency. The working party collected on the west side of the bridge in the best shelter available—a few shattered houses—and to get across to the new position they had to go over in pairs between bursts. Casualties occurred, several were killed and wounded, the new detachment suffering most, maybe because these men didn't seem able to flatten themselves out with the alacrity of the more practised older hands.

Cover in Ypres was very limited, and as it was very difficult to find suitable accommodation in the Cavalry Barracks, a good number of the men were temporarily accommodated in the old shot tower, which had very thick walls and withstood several direct hits. With the scarcity of cover, movement had to be exercised with a certain amount of caution; a "flattening out" was a common occurrence. Capt. Godlee had on one occasion to reprove Lieut. Showan for not falling flat. Lieut. Showan replied in his best droll manner, "If I stand sideways, no shell on earth will hit me."

On the 27th June No. 3 gun was put out of action by enemy shell fire with a damaged recuperator, and two days later Capt. Godlee was wounded and Wheeler Gunner Jimmy Sawer was also wounded by a number of splinters from an H.E. shell which exploded close by.

During one particularly heavy bombardment by the enemy batteries, Lieut. Showan and some of his detachment were "imprisoned" for some hours in one half of an incomplete dug-out—two unfortunate colleagues in the other half. Time was passed telling yarns, so as to keep the party cheerful, all expecting any moment to be the last. After a time Gunner Quigley ventured out, and shortly afterwards returned carrying a dead sparrow, remarking to Lieut. Showan. "There you are, guv'nor—the only ruddy casualty."

The position allotted to us, just in rear of the Cavalry Barracks, was a hopeless one from the point of concealment, as in order to fire over the Cavalry Barracks the guns had to be mounted in an open piece of ground covered with very long grass. The tracks made in getting the guns to their emplacements were naturally very conspicuous from the air, and as nothing could be done which would adequately camouflage them, the whole position could be seen from an enemy sausage balloon which always seemed to be up in the same spot.

As the time for the offensive was approaching, the group had to send a report daily as to how many guns were in "The City," and so in order to enable a report to be made that the requisite number were in "The City" on a certain day, we were ordered to tow up two guns from a position of comparative safety at the rear and leave them close to the wall of the cavalry barracks, even though we were not in a position to mount them, in order that they could be reported as in "The City." About an hour before the big strafe commenced one gun was mounted, and finally all the guns were put up and a few counter battery shoots with aeroplane observation were carried out.

On the evening of the 30th June, whilst an aerial observed shoot was in progress, enemy planes were seen overhead. On this being reported to H.Q. the reply was, "This is a battle operation, on no account cease fire"—so the shoot was therefore continued.

At about 5 a.m. on the 4th July we were detailed for an aeroplane shoot and fired a few rounds, but the visibility was too bad and the aeroplane went home. Later, about 7.30 a.m., the Battery was very heavily shelled by 5.9s. O.K.s were soon obtained on the ammunition, and the position was soon a mass of smoke and flames, approximately 3,000 shells and cartridges exploding during the course of the bombardment. No doubt what actually happened appears to have been that the hostile plane of the previous evening had spotted us firing and had reported the Battery's position, so when this hostile bombardment began a whole string of "sausages" were up, with the morning sun behind them, observing and directing the heavy bombardment of our Battery. Major Cobbold, who had gone to bed after the early morning shoot, hearing the bombardment, went out, and seeing all the ammunition exploding, gave orders for the position to be evacuated, but on returning to the B.C. post was severely wounded. Gunner Martin just escaped by being in front of him.

He was given immediate attention by Gunners Martin and Gardner, together with our medical orderly, "Count Iodine," as we all knew him. Very soon Bentall arrived, and together they lifted Major Cobbold from where he lay just inside the B.C. post in a pool of blood, his leg badly shattered. They managed to get him on to a stretcher and then discovered that the doorway of the B.C. post was too narrow to pass through. So they rolled him off the stretcher as easy and as best they could—doubtless causing him much pain—then carried him through, to load him up again outside.

The little square in front of the Cavalry Barracks wherein the B.C. post was situated was receiving all the shells directed on No. 2 gun, and no sooner had this little rescue party replaced Major Cobbold on the stretcher than a 5.9 burst on the pavé of the square, just missing them, but causing them to drop the Major in a frantic "flop" that was only second nature, especially in Ypres. Although it must have given the Major another cruel shaking it probably saved some lives, and we had none to spare just then ! At any rate, Major Cobbold stood it extremely well, grinned cheerfully, and asked if anyone was hurt. Having assured him in this respect, the party picked themselves up and doubled hell-for-leather across the square, round the corner to the dressing station at the Lille Gate without further mishap. So accurate was the enemy firing that once they got away a little to the left they were all pretty well safe. During the hours that our battery was under this hostile attack, the gallantry of several men, especially Gunner R. Last, cannot be too highly praised. Our casualties that day were heavy—Gunners J. Clelland and B. Hunt were killed and 30 men were wounded, amongst whom were Bombr. R. Hodges, Gunners F. Haldon and F. Faulkner, Bombr. E. F. Miller and Gunner D. A. Marchant, all wounded and taken to hospital.

Lieuts. Starkey and Showan, together with B.S.M. Martin, were the last to leave the battery position, and by good fortune got safely to the shelter of the dug-outs in the ramparts by the Lille Gate, where, with many of our survivors, they were welcomed by the Canadian engineers in charge.

A member of the Battery who had the opportunity later on in the morning of viewing the position, was amazed at what he saw. All the four guns were out of action and Nos. 2 and 3 were practically uprooted, and a huge cavity where the ammunition of the guns had been before it was exploded by the enemy fire. The ground in the front and the rear of each gun was absolutely ploughed up, and in the intervals between the guns there were very few shell holes, which is evidence of the extremely good shooting of the hostile batteries, who it is estimated strafed us with about 1,500 shells from 5.9 upwards.

Lieut. E. Starkey proceeded to collect the men as best he could, found them any available cover in order to rest until the bombardment had ceased.

It was not long, however, before we again were busy, and a position was selected N.W. of Ypres on the Brielen road, in a field behind a row of ruined houses. The "billets" here were chiefly "sandbagged elephants" and disused gun pits—none too sound, but they were sufficient to keep out the rain. Conditions were little different here, and the casualty list continued to grow, the names of

Gunner C. Harley and J. Upham being added on July 10th. Mustard gas, too, took its toll. (It is unfortunate that records are far from complete with regard to all casualties, and unless known all names cannot be mentioned.)

Throughout July, 76 carried on with its work, and continued as successful as ever, in spite of the nasty checks, and during this month A/Cpl. A. Raeburn, Gunners H. Jones, R. Wakefield and "Nigger" Conquest were killed, whilst the following were wounded or gassed and left the Battery : "Busty" Gardner, Newson, Bombr. Jack Fisher, Charlie Meekins and Penstone (Pen). Many others suffered from gas and were sent down the line, and never returned to the Battery strength.

And so with time and the ravages of war, the Battery began fast to lose old familiar faces, but with reinforcements from the base the good work carried on, and promotion was of necessity much quicker.

What is hereafter recorded must in consequence be a narrative drawn from personal recollections and diaries supplied by survivors of 76; there being no continuing surviving officer a continuous record is impossible.

In spite of these conditions the gun teams, each admirably led by their respective No. 1, worked as well as ever, giving untold energy and valued assistance in maintaining the high standard of accuracy of fire. Sergt. Willis earned great respect as he, notably, bore the brunt of the work, and under frightful conditions stood as much as any human possibly could do.

Towards the end of July, owing to an advance, we moved to Gibraltar Farm, on the left of Potijze village, in a hollow to the right of St. Jean, a spot known to the Boche. Rear billets were found at the "siege" park for reliefs, but gun teams, signallers, staff, etc., were billeted close to the position, which was in a boggy field where 60 pounders and field guns lined the remnants of hedges, whilst the "heavies" sat down where they could. The only remnants of the farm were a few bits of sandbagged brick wall which served as the B.C. post.

By sheer hard work, the pieces having to be man-handled into position, the tractors being unable to get right up to the field and with some pieces sinking into the mud and having to be "tackled" out, four guns were eventually put up in position by August 6th and were in action. The column still brought up the ammunition at night if allowed by hostile batteries, who delighted in strafing the roads. Our transport men suffered casualties on these trips, and realized that motoring wasn't always a "joy-ride." They certainly put up a splendid performance, for the roads were very difficult to drive along. The ammunition had to be dumped by the roadside some distance from the guns, and to avoid rolling the shells through the mud, a Decauville track was laid through the middle of the field on a track of sand which naturally showed up in a contrast of colour, and undoubtedly gave enemy observers an idea to introduce little area shoots. These often lasted for an hour or two and were the very devil, for it seemed that on these occasions the Boche turned all his available 4.2 guns on to this spot. Fortunately the boggy nature of the ground seemed to deprive the shells of some of their power, penetration being deeper and splinters more confined, otherwise our casualties might have been heavier.

The gun teams deserved full praise for their stout work. Rolling ammunition in muddy surroundings and digging satisfactory gun pits in the same soft mud was no easy task, a task perhaps enough to damp the spirits of the strongest —even without the "little area shellings"—but 76 kept at it as best they could, taking part in most stunts and offensive moves, trusting that each push would bring nearer the end of the horrible business.

Another offensive was about to take place, for we fired many rounds per gun all day. Walking wounded and the ambulances which passed down the road, together with many prisoners, also showed signs of "something doing".

On 21st July, 1917, Major Wakeford arrived to take over command of the Battery, and another new officer, Captain G. L. Andrews, arrived. Fresh faces seemed to turn up every day, and very few of the original 76 men appeared to be left.

On 27th July, 1917, Bombr. A. Bentall was awarded the Military Medal for gallantry and devotion to duty. About this time Bentall went on leave, and his departure was marked by the following humorous experience which he tells below in his own words.

"Came heaven in the guise of my first leave after sixteen months in the line, for after various postponements I actually had the little green pass in my hand, and so about 10 p.m. one glorious August evening, all poshed up and dressed like the proverbial Christmas tree, I left the B.S.M.'s office for Blighty, but reckoned without the the B.S.M.'s 'private office,' a typical Belgian cesspool, four to five feet deep. Taking a sudden step in the wrong direction I unhappily found myself well in, up to the armpits, and I can yet see my kit floating away on the 'beastly tide.' 'Ginger' Browne, who was a witness, almost curled up with laughter, and when he had recovered his normal face and I my 'natural' breath, I ventured back to B.S.M. Martin, feeling very much like a bad dog with my tail 'tween my legs, expecting him also to enjoy the joke of my misfortune. Strange to say, he was neither mirthful nor yet officious—just genuinely concerned, so much so that he even offered to rig me out in some of the breeches he kept to impress other B.S.M.s. I would gratefully have borrowed them, but not wishing to feel all bags and being unable to see over the top of them, I had to decline with thanks. I dared not waste one precious minute, so just as I was—collecting Fred Durrant and losing him again—I went off, eventually reaching Poperinghe Station, my spirits, like my clothes, still 'high.' Here I cashed my pay warrant, also Freddy's, which was in my care, and once more started to hunt for him. At last I found him, and never have I seen anyone so pleased to see me, before or since. Trouble, however, still haunted us, for owing to shelling the leave train started some miles down the line, towards Abeele. We were already late, and the little red light of the end carriage seemed but a will of the wisp as we scrambled, rattling, sweating and cursing, over sleepers for what seemed miles. Arrived at last in time, we boarded the train, and thanks to the 'bouquet du Sergt.-Major,' I think, I got plenty of room on that train. What the other 39 'Hommes' thought I know not, nor do I care, for I enjoyed a wonderful leave ere I returned from a peaceful Essex farm to that not-so-peaceful little estate at Gibraltar Farm.''

Now in August we were still very busily engaged, with seldom any rest, and during the second week intensive preparations were made for a determined attack on Zonnebeke, and on the 15th and 16th the Battery still plugged away at our old targets. Conferences took place at group headquarters and officers were selected as forward observation officers who were given stations to which to make their way prior to the attack, with instructions to keep in touch with the infantry and with Group Headquarters by telephone, by wireless and by pigeons, which as far as our observation officer knows, were then supplied for the first time to forward observation officers of the heavy artillery. So on the 16th, a party of signallers, with some men from Headquarters with pigeons, led by Lieut. Showan, set out to take up a position in a pill box near Station House, at the top of the ridge looking down on Zonnebeke. There they joined forces with a subaltern from a 6 inch battery, who reported with his signallers and pigeons. Homing pigeons for each officer's party had been provided, and later they became very useful, as it was found impossible to keep the line to H.Q. alive for more than , five minutes together. In this attack more and more reliance was placed by both sides on directed mass artillery fire, so as to economize in men, for at last the drain on the infantry, caused by pouring over battalions of men, had been realized. At zero hour it was a ghastly sight to see both the enemy and our own first and second line trenches simply blown to pieces by well-directed raking bombardments.

The result was checkmate. The Royal Irish Rifles

below our O.P. were wiped out in two to three minutes, and only a few wounded straggled back. Our pill box offered them shelter, but soon became a shambles.

Even had the lines to H.Q. lived, it would have been useless in such a bombardment, so the pigeons became invaluable, and H.Q. were kept informed by this method of the progress of the infantry operations and of the results of the firing. Our F.O.O. was able about 9 a.m. to round up about 20 straggling Germans who were made to give assistance to our wounded, and who were marched off as stretcher bearers carrying wounded infantry down the slope in the direction of Ypres.

Observation was continued throughout the day and our party remained on duty. Throughout the night the observation party from 76, together with many other similar parties, kept watch and reported at intervals to H.Q. At night the enemy sent over a mixed barrage of gas and high explosives all round the O.P., whereupon the small number remaining on duty took refuge in a broken down tank in front of the O.P., and this afforded a welcome shelter for the time. At dawn, however, the enemy decided to destroy the tank, which made a difference to the small party inside the target. Fortunately, however, though some "Ys" and "Zs" were registered on the unhappy occupants, no actual O.K. arrived before the small party were able to make a hasty and undignified exit.

. Later that day the F.O.O. and men of 76 Siege were relieved from further duty by H.Q., and returned to the Battery. On reporting to H.Q., however, Lieut. Showan was gassed and hurried off to hospital. (Next day in hospital he was wounded during an air raid on the hospital, and was evacuated to England.)

Hostile shelling was still frequent in the neighbourhood of the Battery, and the casualty list was still growing. Gunner Gabriel was killed on the 21st August, and gas and wounds were the cause of others leaving. On one of these occasions a shell landed in "C" gun pit between the gun and the earth box, luckily only tilting the gun, but causing more work and cursing getting it put back again. The boggy nature of the earth was responsible for a new stunt with more digging, tree trunks as heavy as the baulks themselves being laid to make a foundation for the latter to rest on. Firing at points in Zonnebeke, in front of Passchendaele and much counter battery work was the order of the day, and we found this position very wretched for the Germans knew it very well and seldom left us alone.

Time passed on, Major Wakeford doing his best with a sadly-reduced complement of officers and men, for apart from casualties, two sections went out on a much-needed rest to a camp at Poperinghe. Conditions seemed to get worse. The constant shelling was a menace, and "C" gun was once again unlucky, for a shell landed in the gun pit when the team were all present and on duty. Sergt. Barnes 1/C was unhurt, but Runnacles, Durrant and a few others were wounded and taken to the dressing station; from there some of them were sent to "Blighty." Happily, however, at this position we had rear billets when off duty, and though not far away from the Battery position it provided some small consolation when the turn came for the detachments to take a bit of rest and sleep.

It was a strange 76, on reflection. The old familiar faces seemed so few, as most of the "old" boys had been either killed, wounded, transferred, etc. Captain Ted Starkey was the only one of the original officers now left, and he began to look almost "all-in," and no surprise, for he spent much of his time at those unhealthy places, "O-Pips."

These "O-Pips" supplied little cover, and on September 24th at one of these places, merely a small concrete shelter, Gunner "Bill" Buckoke lost his life, being killed instantly by a shell which struck the back of the shelter. As one of the signallers on duty, he was standing outside in the shallow trench, and had no chance whatever. Buckoke was a most likeable chap, always laughing or singing—he possessed quite a good tenor voice—and his death came as a great shock. This same day Gunner H. W. Stephenson was also killed.

Two days later a move was made, "C" and "D" guns having to go to a position at the top of a sloping field off Cambridge Road, very exposed, whilst "A" and "B" guns went to the White Château. Pulling out through the night, moving by night, dig, dig, dig, the same old mud and slime, eventually in position again and firing, the same old conditions, same hostile strafing. Here there were dug-outs, a few, but rather frail, sufficient to keep the clothes dry from the rain, and perhaps a small comfort to know the head was covered, and whilst there was in some cases a duck-board for a bed which *might* clear the water underneath, the best use of ground sheets had to be made for a "kip."

The Germans spotted our Decauville railway and shelled with a long range H.V. gun. Our rear billets being in line got some too, and one or two gunners were killed. J. Whitehouse, officers' cook, is believed to be one, and a few others were wounded; consequent upon such happenings, the strain kept telling, several men going on the sick list and having to be replaced. Apart from the usual daily orders of bombardment, we had much S.O.S. work at night, and in response to these calls by the infantry, had to turn out and let off bursts of fire, and with sadly-depleted gun teams this was no easy task, and the *morale* of the men was severely tested.

However, the Battery retained as much spirit as was humanly possible, and still had a "kick" in them, as the following incident proved. The usually little party of observers and signallers were at the O.P. where Buckoke lost his life, Lieut. Irwine in charge. Visibility was good, a sunny afternoon, with the Boche still holding Passchendaele village and the slope for some distance in front of it. The party were witnessing the customary desultory strafe of the enemy support area on the slope, the ruins of the church plainly visible on the top of the ridge. Noticing a flash in the orchard to the west of the village, Lieut. Irwine suddenly exclaimed, "What is that? Maybe shrapnel a little further over, no doubt." "No it isn't, it's a hostile battery, by jove!'' "The cheek of it—in full view, too; they must think we're pretty slack," but they reckoned without 76.

O.P. to Battery : "Enemy battery in action (map reference), 2 degrees left of Passchendaele church from O.P.''

O.C. 76 : "Oh, there is, is there. Right! Stand by for our first round.''

At the O.P. the party anxiously waited, and following the first round or two all guns were soon ranged, the church serving as a perfect point for switching. Very soon 76 are sending over a direct supply of a different kind of "fruit" in that orchard, and within a few minutes a huge column of black smoke shoots up from amongst the trees whilst through their glasses our observers see bursts of flame—76 fairly got on to that battery's ammunition. Battery and gun fire continued for some time, until the observers were satisfied that that hostile battery were out of action, and as long as our party remained at the O.P. no firing came from that direction, at any rate.

One night in early October in response to an S.O.S. at midnight, rain teeming down and pitch dark, and with but four to five men on each gun, the B.C.'s assistant gave the line as ordered to each gun in turn. Coming to No. 4 gun someone said, "Who's going to lay the b—— gun, then?'' That gun's crew consisted of about four men, no N.C.O. or gun layer. Never having laid a gun before, the B.C.A. did so, and "cocking her up" well, gave the order "Fire," trusting all would be well and wondering, "Where did that one go to!''

October 6th was a bad day for 76, as after he had ranged with a few tracers, Jerry eventually sent over a few rounds between the two "C" and "D" guns. A few more were killed, names unknown, and wounded. Amongst the former was one unfortunate known as "Deadwood Dick," who had had a job at the rear billets as the "rear wallah." Owing to shortage of men the B.S.M. had sent him up to the Battery, and so, on his first day on the guns, he met his end. Poor chap, he was a man over fifty with a big family.

Rumours of being relieved of our guns gave rise to hopes of a change. A Canadian battery came and took over, and 76 went back, leaving behind one officer and two other ranks. But two days later, back came 76 with *buttons* cleaned, after a short rest, to take back from the Canadians —so the change was very short-lived.

October dragged along. The ammunition was a big difficulty, nothing was orderly (what would Mr. Sandercock have said?), just one big heap of shells, and we took them as we wanted them. We got more stunts at night : very rarely did a night pass without everybody having to turn out. If it wasn't for ammunition, then it was an S.O.S. or one of those desultory "so many rounds an hour stunts."

Towards the end of October another move was made forward to Frezenburg Ridge—and once again we found ourselves in a "nice" spot. Just as muddy and just as "hot" as Gibraltar Farm, but fortunately once again we had rear billets which, whilst being still in the danger zone, were sufficiently far enough back to give one that (perhaps false) sense of security and rest. Here again the method of transporting the inevitable ammunition to the guns was by means of the famous Decanville railway with trucks. But the "rolling stock" here apparently was never passed by the Board of Trade, for the trucks seemed top heavy. In fact, the sides overlapped, and if by chance, and it often happened, the truck was loaded too much on one side, over went the lot, and many a shell has been written off amongst the "expended" while they lay, and may still lie, at the bottom of a shell hole alongside the track. Occasional passes to Poperinghe were granted, and these provided a little relief from the daily routine and hostile shelling, if only for a few hours.

The opportunity of a good feed, a drink or two, and a stroll round Pop was a welcome sedative. Taking advantage of this privilege, Gunner Joe Lambert and a friendly Bombardier enjoyed themselves very well one afternoon and returned late in the evening.

In luck's way they are given a lift on a lorry whose driver said he was going to "Vlam." Having "dined" well in Pop, the two artillerymen doze for a little. Suddenly awaking, the Bombardier peers out and sees the ruined church tower of Vlamentinghe looking a bit ghostly in the moonlight, and standing up above the ground mist which had gathered. "Here we are, Joe, out you get." Both scrambled out, and the N.C.O. proceeded to take his bearings.

The fog getting thicker didn't help much, but still, for all that, the way seemed strangely unfamiliar. After several "casts" to find the road to the rear billets at St. Jean, the following conversation took place.

Bombr. : "Joe, do you know where we are?"

Joe : "You said it's Vlam !"

Bombr. : "Well, it isn't. This is Elverdinghe."

Joe (in his best bass guffaw) : "You're a ruddy fine B.C.A., you are !'

Continuing their trek through the fog miles across country, with a little welcome interlude at an E.F. Canteen, the two eventually arrived at St. Jean, where the Bombardier goes up to the Sergeants' Mess to report their return to the Sergt.-Major. Unknown to the Bombardier, Joe Lambert stands behind him in the doorway making signs to the Sergt.-Major.

Bombr. : "Have just come to report back, Sergt.-Major."

Sergt.-Major (who has doubtless done himself fairly well and is nicely mellow) : "Bent, you're drunk."

And so Joe got his own back.

Another offensive took place and a further success by our infantry helped along the progress in this sector, and drove back the German right flank. We ourselves were engaged in many heavy bombardments, intermingled with counter battery work.

Following a hostile air raid, in which bombs were dropped close to the rear billets, a further calamity befell the Battery. During enemy strafing, a shell fell on a dug-out of "A" section, many men being killed, amongst whom were Gunners A. Paternoster, A. Burton, F. Ormerod and T. Jones. Other names are not known, but it is known that Gunner "Woodrow" Wilson did excellent work assisting in the removal of the wounded, for which he was awarded the Military Medal on 24th November, 1917.

A few days later, while in action, 76 were again shelled. One enemy shell landed close to one of our guns. Sergt. Bill Willis, No. 1 of the gun, had a lucky escape, but Gunners H. W. Cope and A. Ashhurst received very bad wounds, from which they died later.

It was fortunate for the Battery, as Sergt. Willis was one whom we could not spare. Bill embodied all that was desired—a fine sergeant and No. 1, who could always get the best out of his men in a persuasive way entirely his own, and above all, most cool and courageous throughout these trying days.

November arrived cold and very rainy, the wheeler gunner very busy making little crosses for the unfortunate ones. It was an eerie task, full of pain, constructing a small but honoured monument to each one : a pal here, and there another, also a member of 76, yet a comparative stranger, this a result of so many casualties and hurried reinforcements. Constant changing, new faces arriving, old ones departing, a sad picture of 76 as we knew it in its palmy days. Though but few of the original men of 76 were actually killed, they diminished, either wounded, gassed or sick, and it became a remnant of its former self.

On 12th November, 1917, the Battery again were pleased to hear that Gunners N. Quigley and S. Cooper had been awarded the Military Medal for devotion to duty and gallantry under shell fire.

Four days later, 16th November, Capt. E. D. R. Ramsdale, of 333 Siege Battery, was posted to 76 as second in command.

Although we continued to carry on with the daily round of tasks, firing, fatigues, digging, etc., little was actually known of what was going on—what battle or offensive was taking place—for there seemed to be an absence of news, "official" news. So unlike the old days on the Somme, when Corps, or even group, news was circulated. An occasional copy of the "Daily Mail" was often the only means of knowing how the war was going on. Doubtless the officers knew more, but amongst the men little news got round.

The position at Frezenburg Ridge was not at all pleasant, the weather was wretched and conditions beyond description. The dumping of ammunition became a task nearly beyond endurance, and the B.C.A. found it almost impossible to check the rounds and keep accurate returns.

When December arrived the Battery moved again, and all guns were put up along the Godley road. Beyond the usual round of targets, trenches, strong points, emplacements, etc., and occasional counter battery work, there is very little to relate. Casualties continued to be fairly heavy, Gunners A. Crampin and P. Tate being amongst those known killed, whilst many others were wounded or fell sick, Gunner M. Turner being amongst the latter.

As the month wore on things quietened down a bit, and one gained a little more ease and time for reflection. It really seemed as if the authorities had at last decided that Flanders mud could swallow up more men than they could ever produce.

Christmas came again, but it was a sadder one this time; we had little time for "jollity or fun," and many felt depressed and weary.

With the arrival of the New Year, 1918, conditions improved, better and more comfortable rear billets were obtained; and soon after the Battery moved to Steenworde to enjoy a well-earned rest. Here there were civilian people, cafés which supplied a pleasant change from the usual field rations, eggs and chips, and the opportunity of a glass of beer or wine were luxuries enjoyed by all. This rest undoubtedly proved of great benefit to the Battery as a whole, and when in February we were ordered to move south, where a "big push" was taking place, everyone was refreshed and elated, the fighting spirit stimulated. Which way the "push" was didn't concern 76, for uppermost in the minds of all was the desire to leave "The Salient," of which we had had more than enough for a lifetime. In lovely weather the Battery journeyed South by easy stages, travelling well behind the line, once more into the Somme area, and by the time we arrived at Morlancourt we had almost forgotten the war.

Major Wakeford gave a sum of money for sport, and after a certain amount of travelling, footballs and football boots were obtained, and the Battery once more found a good team from its personnel. Goalposts were needed, and having once seen some in a field near an E.F.C. canteen, a corporal went off with a lorry, loaded up the posts, the property of the canteen, and then invited the canteen to find a team to play 76. The match was arranged, and the goalposts remained with the Battery until broken up by shell fire on the morning of 21st March, 1918. By now there were still about thirty of the original Battery left, and naturally all of them were very pally and felt quite veterans.

CHAPTER V.

1918. THE SOMME AGAIN.
RETREAT—ADVANCE—ARMISTICE.

By the third day of March the Battery was once again
on the move, and after a two days' journey through
Combles, Trones Wood, Montauban, Sailly Sallisel, the
Battery eventually reached Hermies.
The gun position selected was in a disused quarry on
the Ruyaulcourt road, not far from the main Bapaume-
Cambrai road, and to a certain extent it was an ideal spot,
with one fairly safe dug-out which may have at one time
housed some of the Boche. But as the quarry faced the
German line, all the openings and doors we constructed
made things none too comfortable, though such difficulties
we had experienced before. One casualty had to be reported here, that of Gunner "Trunky" Barton, the
Battery's amateur barber, who was wounded.
During a week of digging-in, assisted by a party of
Australian miners, three guns, by reason of being parallel
with our line of fire, were put down in a line one behind the
other, this method being rather unorthodox and strange
to the ideas put forward at lectures. The reason was
largely due to the fact of the quarry being dug along the
side of the road, which road coincided with the line of fire.
In any case, the guns were far enough apart so as not to
cause inconvenience to the crews ahead when firing took
place. Following registration of the guns, very little shooting took place and an order eventually came along with instructions "not to shoot," as rumours were around
that an enemy offensive was in the offing, but when, no one
knew. Such is rumour, and what rumours can we all recall !
So for a short time there was little for the men to do,
though, of course, as usual the signallers were busy lay-

ing lines to various O.P.s, etc., but even they found time to relax with the rest, and the football gear came out again.

It all seemed so strange, judging by the small amount of action on the part of ourselves and the Boche, especially after having just left Ypres, where the "fireworks" were so plentiful and cheap. Duties at the O.P. were quite pleasant, and from front line trenches it was easy to watch the activities of the enemy, and, of course, with the aid of glasses it was possible to see him getting guns into position.

Conditions were ideal here for about three weeks, no firing, and football practically all day long, officers and men enjoying the games, played on a full-sized pitch which was only marred by one shell hole, which we had, of course, filled in and levelled.

But with the inactivity and lack of hostility a certain ominous feeling gathered, for it began to be imagined that perhaps Jerry had our position taped and was only marking time. Our football he must have seen, for the field was very exposed—maybe he was waiting and getting his "shooting boots" on, and to show what the German "Arsenal" could do.

These fears were unfortunately only too soon realized, for on the 21st of March a short while before daybreak, somewhere about 4 a.m., the alarm was sounded to the gun crews to go into action on S.O.S. lines, and very soon the Battery was blazing away. The Boche retaliated heavily. The first damage was to the football pitch, and those posts we had so recently "borrowed" were smashed up and unreturnable. Conditions became almost indescribable. H.E. shrapnel and gas seemed to fill the air. Gas masks had to be hastily donned, and under this extra handicap it became extremely difficult to man the guns, and of all, the gun layers had the hardest task on account of the eye-pieces of the gas masks getting misty with moisture. At times they had to risk a lift of the mask in order that the rate and accuracy of fire should be maintained. For a time the reply to the S.O.S. had to be abandoned, but when the hostile strafing had ceased our action continued, although No. 1 gun was completely out of action and most of the ammunition the worse for wear.

During the early stages of this strafe many enemy planes were up and doing damage to and bringing down our balloons, causing one "eye" of the guns to be closed, and strangely enough our R.F.C. did not appear.

As the day wore on we found ourselves in a sorry plight, but still we remained in action. A gas shell landed on Major Wakeford's dug-out. The B.C.A.—Fred Abbott— had gone to phone H.Q., at the wish of the O.C., and returned to find him suffering from wounds which proved fatal a few hours later; another officer was also killed on this day, during which our casualties were pretty heavy. So we were temporarily without an O.C. (Captain Ramsdale, next in command, being at the base on a course).

Infantry falling back related stories of the extent of the German advance, where they were, and what they had gained. Later in the day Major Ramsdale arrived to take over command of the Battery, and gave the order to pull out, which came as no surprise, but much to the relief of the Battery, and very soon the A.S.C.M.T. arrived with lorries and tractors, and the work of pulling out was in full swing, and through working into the night, the guns and some, not all, stores were got out in record time. All messes were cleared, and a store of rum and whisky was distributed, to the satisfaction of many. One man had one regret—Dan Rose had to leave behind a nice German waterproof valise and a feather pillow which he had treasured, in spite of sarcastic remarks, for two whole years —a sad loss to Dan.

Lack of communication or ability to get in touch with Group H.Q. caused much difficulty, and early morning found the Battery in retreat—the first in its experience. Before the last remnants of stores left, the enemy were already in occupation of Hermies village. The R.F.A. had already gone back past our quarries, as also had many of our infantry. After a terribly slow journey, we eventually got back to Ruyaulcourt, the Battery's reserve position, where the three remaining guns were emplaced. Soon we were busy digging positions for the retreating guns from the quarries, lorries being sent back for fresh baulks to replace those left behind. On their arrival the guns were mounted, the task being completed by the evening of March 22nd. It was all, however, "Love's labour lost," for shortly after the guns were up the order to "pull out" came, but as no firing had taken place there was no rear or side tilt, so the task was easier.

During the various stages of the retreat the Battery cooks worked splendidly, if not heroically, to do all they possibly could, regardless both of the bombardment and the inconvenience. Daybreak of the 23rd found the Battery on the move again to another spot at Les Mesnil, near Bus, and once more gun pits were dug for our third position in 48 hours. The digging proceeded and baulks were put down, and guns were in various stages of mounting when at noon the order to quit once again came through, and it was at this stage evidently that someone in authority had suddenly realized that 9.2 howitzers, being only semi-mobile, were of no use in a running battle. The orders now were to get right out of the way, and so with the guns being only partially mounted the Battery was soon packed up and off again, back through Bapaume and on to Albert, our original starting point in 1916.

Transport, however, was extremely slow and difficult owing to congestion of traffic of all kinds, infantry, wagons, guns, etc., and the task of piloting a 9.2 howitzer battery along under such conditions was by no means easy, especially under pressure of the enemy advance. On the road back we passed through Rocquigny, where our A.S.C. column had been billeted, and it was with gratitude we received some welcome tea that they served out as we passed.

Passing through Bapaume we found the town being heavily shelled and it became a matter of "running the gauntlet." Conditions were terrible, and the congestion, bombs and shell fire made getting through the town that night an experience that those who were with the Battery will never forget. There was such chaos in the traffic that the Battery became split up into a number of sub units, each being unaware of the fate of the rest. A number of casualties occurred in Bapaume, and a little way outside the town on the road to Albert, Gunner Cruise, dead-beat and dozing, fell off the caterpillar tractor on which he was riding, beneath the wheel of the following gun—a very sad end.

Reviewing the whole of the events of this retreat on the lighter side, we found that the country through which we travelled back was not too badly scarred by shell fire; we even found some vegetables growing which provided an addition to the menu. The "scroungers" got busy, and there were many varied meals prepared by amateur cooks with the aid of iron rations and the newly-found vegetables. Steak, chips and cabbage seemed to be most popular and, although cooked in the crudest fashion, were wholeheartedly enjoyed. Hastily vacated houses, odd shops, and, best of all, B.E.F. canteens left to their fate, provided many a bottle of wine and a few other luxuries.

Memories of 1916 and the First Battle of the Somme were revived as the Battery passed back along the Bapaume road, Martinpuich, Pozieres with Spring Gardens and across the valley Ovillers, all positions where eighteen months ago we were doing so well, full of zeal and enthusiasm over the Somme advance, and now, though still in good spirits, to return in retreat perhaps created a deep feeling of dejection amongst those of 76 who still survived, and were able to recall those early days.

The split in traffic had caused a delay of four to five hours between the "van" and the "rear" units of the Battery over a distance of 20 miles, which showed how slowly we had progressed. After a few hours' sleep and breakfast, the Battery arrived at Albert, where again a rich haul was made by some of the "enterprising scouts" who salvaged an abandoned lorry loaded with such dainties as lobster, biscuits, wine, fruit, etc., which provided some good fare for at least a few more days.

At Albert, for the first time for many a day, we were in contact with French civilians who were retreating and busy gathering together what household effects and treasures they could possibly manage to place on their various forms of transport : some horse drawn, others with hand carts, the womenfolk in the shafts—and the less fortunate with crude types of barrows and bundles. In many cases the family cow was present, either being towed or led behind. A motley tragic throng, which only served to remind us of our own folk at home, and make us thankful that they were at least housed, and not harassed and homeless like these poor unfortunates. Albert itself had changed somewhat from the place we had known it to be in 1916. Many of the old ruins were the same, but in quite a few places new buildings had been erected during the days after the Boche had been driven back in March, 1917. But such is the fortune of war, these new buildings were not to last long, as events subsequently proved.

Picking up the threads of the story once again, the battery found billets near the town in an old château which was not too badly damaged, and a general hope was fostered that the stay here would not be too short. Rest and sleep were most urgently needed by all officers and men of the Battery after the most strenuous hardships of the previous few days, during which they had only been able to snatch a few hours' sleep from the early morning of Thursday 21st to Sunday 24th.

Albert town itself was put out of bounds, though this did not prevent a venturesome few paying a visit to Albert. They almost landed themselves in disaster as a certain Colonel, who was actively engaged in the town collecting stragglers of all units and forming an emergency corps, commandeered them into his corps, and it needed much persuasion on the part of those venturesome fellows before the Colonel could be made to understand that our Battery would be hopeless without them. He eventually let them go, and they were thus spared having to carry rifles and bombs.

The Battery did not stay long in the Albert vicinity, and the hopes of a position being taken, and perhaps also some much-needed rest, did not materialize, for it became known during the morning of March the 24th that a concentrated attack by air was to be launched by the Boche, and orders were given that the town, and the immediate vicinity, be evacuated without delay. Soon everything was once again packed up, and the Battery was on the move, and once out of the town parked for a few hours in a field alongside the Albert-Bouzincourt road, where all who could took advantage of the chance of a rest, but this was rudely disturbed by the air attack which took place very shortly after our parking here. It proved to be a very vicious attack, the bombing being incessant and severe; much damage was done, so that the Battery were perhaps fortunate to move when it did.

After a few hours' stay, orders were received to proceed, so we set off through Bouzincourt on to Forceville, where near by the town a halt was called in the early hours of the 25th March. A short rest and some breakfast was taken before a further move was made, this time back again to Bouzincourt, and a general impression was gathered that the enemy advance had been checked. It is believed that a move was started from here due to orders alleged to have been given by a German spy. Some batteries were actually on their way but were eventually stopped. The Battery remained inactive for the rest of the day—bombs could still be heard bursting in Albert, and some men from the Battery who made a quick visit to the town, saw some terrible sights, the result of the previous day's air attack. Terrific damage had been done, and there had been much loss of life.

During the late evening everybody was on parade again, and yet another move took place, travelling over the same road as before, but this time right through to Doullens. Such was the state of apprehension on this occasion, the rear

F

lorries were manned by gunners with Lewis guns, in case the column should be overtaken by Germany Cavalry. So cold was the weather that many preferred to walk beside the guns and tractors rather than ride, in order to keep warm. All through the night the Battery travelled, and at daybreak were still some miles away from the town, but with steady progress Doullens was reached, and we passed through before the town was awake.

Here again old memories were revived for a few of us of the time when back in 1916 we were practically all new to it, lighthearted and fresh, detraining our guns on their arrival from Boulogne, for our trip up to the line. What a waste of time and energy it all seemed now, back once again where we started, and maybe yet to go back further —who was to know?

Passing on, and leaving Doullens and its memories behind us, we headed for the Abbeville road, and eventually came to rest at the small village of Hem, a veritable sanctuary after the hell we had recently experienced. This little place proved to be our final stop in the retreat. Our stay here came as a great relief to all, for we had travelled back something over 40 miles from Hermies, which we evacuated on the night of the 21st/22nd March, and had been almost constantly retreating from that time till about 7 p.m. on the 26th.

It had been a very trying and tiring time, and the personnel of the Battery deserved much credit for the manner in which they all endured the hardships of the journey. Mention must also be made of the magnificent work of the A.S.C. column, for both the lorry and the caterpillar sections carried out their tasks splendidly. Every move at all times depended on them, and too much praise cannot be extended to them for the part they played throughout the retreat. Few will forget the red-hot exhausts of the tractors emitting showers of sparks during the dash through Bapaume under shell fire; also the speed with which they started up and got the column moving when orders were received to move on. Their kindly actions, too, in giving us a lift on the lorries for a little rest during the retreat, and their provision of extra rations now and again, formed but a small part of their unstinted comradeship which we shall always remember and appreciate.

As we did not know when we arrived whether we should remain at Hem or not, very little was done. No official billets were provided, and the men slept wherever they could : this proved in most cases to be out in the open. Some were fortunate to find shelter in the hedgerows, though on account of the bitterly cold, frosty weather very few found much comfort.

The following day, however, billets were obtained in farm buildings, and in the luxury of newly-acquired straw, early retirements were the order, and indeed it would have taken many a bomb to disturb our heavy slumbers. Breakfast here could be augmented by fresh eggs in plenty, provided that one rose early *and* before the farmer.

The stay at Hem lasted nearly a fortnight, and as there was little to be done, the quietness and rest were greatly enjoyed by all. Apart from the ordinary fatigues, our work mainly consisted of work on the guns, which were mounted, cleaned and dismounted, exercises which afforded a useful bit of practice, especially for the reinforcements which had arrived.

Frequent passes to Doullens were available, and much advantage was taken of this privilege, which enabled members of the Battery to get a little welcome relaxation and pleasure, for though the Boche planes bombed the town almost every night, they did not cause us any particular worry. Fortunately the bombing did not reach as far as Hem, so the nights were passed without anxiety or interruption of rest. As the days passed by, it became a topic of conversation as to when a move would be made and to where.

The move eventually started on April 11th, when three guns were moved up to Herissart, roughly ten miles west of Albert. Digging commenced, firing beams were laid, and with much hard work the three guns were got into the position, but no firing took place as the spot was too far back. It may be that step was precautionary in the event of a further sudden break through by the Germans, but fortunately, however, no further advance was made by the enemy, and after a week's stay at Herissart, the three guns were dismounted and proceeded to Forceville, where upon the arrival of the remainder of the Battery from Hem a position was taken up in a cornfield on the Varennes road. Once in position we at last got into action and got through quite a lot of firing, but although we received a little strafing occasionally, things were not too bad, and as the weather had improved conditions became much more possible.

The next move was not long delayed, for the German offensive had about reached its limit (perhaps even over-reached it) and it was found possible to get a little closer to the newly-formed line with our heavy guns without running too much risk of losing them. So early in May the other three guns were put in position at Mailly-Maillet wood. As the road was heavily shelled the journey there was not without excitement, and it was a real struggle to get through. Good luck was with us, however, and there were no casualties to report when we reached our destination.

From many points of view the position seemed ideal. Trees gave a certain amount of cover from both aerial and ground observation, whilst a bank in front was the means of obtaining shelter. The bank was sapped at intervals and dug-outs constructed, and a certain sense of security was obtained by such cover, but it caused a good deal of toil, for sapping is much harder work than digging into the loose soil. Still, the work was eventually finished and the cover obtained was appreciated in many ways. But the ideal position notion was soon lost, for we received a fair amount of strafing, which perhaps one really ought to have expected, for there is no doubt that the wood raised a certain amount of suspicion and soon became an object of attention.

The first casualties were caused when a dud shell arrived and crashed in a dug-out and buried a number of men. A party at once proceeded to dig them out, and though most were got out alive, some were wounded and two, unfortunately, were dead. It was understood that the act of rescue was treated as a case of collective gallantry under shell fire, and Lieut. Grange was awarded the M.C., Sergt. Semple the D.C.M., and Sergt. Mudge the M.M. Later the Battery again received recognition in the honours list, 2nd Lieut. H. L. Johnston being awarded the Military Cross during April, 1918.

Included amongst these hostile shell attacks there was much gas, and this caused not only a lot of inconvenience but considerable danger, and it was some time before masks could be discarded following an attack of this nature.

On May 22nd the Battery suffered heavy losses during a hostile bombardment by the enemy, 20 men being killed and 13 wounded.

Day by day much firing was done from this position, and to "ease" things a little the gun teams were periodically changed over, Mailly-Maillet to Forceville and vice versa. With Forceville reckoned as the "rear" position, things were a little quieter there and allowed those on duty a little relaxation, even an occasional game of cricket with neighbouring batteries. The wicket (?) was situated in front of two 9 inch long-range guns on railway mountings, and it seemed to amuse their crews to open up when a game was in progress. Maybe they thought an over or two of fast stuff was necessary ! Unfortunately it caused "Jerry" to take a hand in the game sometimes, and as a consequence play was held up or abandoned—one might almost say "Heavy" rain stopped play.

About this time Captain Andrews joined the strength, but unfortunately his stay was of a very short duration, for he was killed soon afterwards whilst on the way to the O.P. with Lieut. Godlee and Signaller Jones. Lieut. Godlee, who had rejoined the Battery only three weeks previously

—after being in hospital in England recovering from his previous wound—and Jones were seriously wounded. (A/Capt. Godlee returned to 76 as Lieutenant during April, 1918.) Shortly after, orders were received from Corps H.Q. notifying the posthumous award of the M.C. to the late Major Wakeford.

Many men seemed at this time to be affected by a kind of influenza or fever. The general opinion formed was that it was in fact actually a fever, the cause being due to the heavy shelling disturbing much of the decomposed remains in the area, which was, of course, the scene of so much carnage in the Somme offensive in 1916.

The Battery continued to run these two positions for quite a considerable time, June and July passing with the usual routine, and taking part in the programme of suppressing the enemy and assisting in the recovery of lost ground by our infantry. Slowly the upper hand was gained, and with the consolidation of these little gains there came a time, mid-way through August, when it was decided that our Forceville position was practically useless now that defence was no longer the main issue for us. The turning point evidently had been reached, as we shortly discovered, for it was "offence" both day and night in the very near future.

(Lack of records between August 19th and the middle of September must of necessity cause a break in the record as to what took place, but as far as can be gathered a position at Engelbelmer was worked on, but vacated without a gun being mounted. The opening of the Allied offensive caused many hurried moves—one to Mesnil near Hamel, then on to Bellacourt.)

From the position at Bellacourt the Battery moved out to a camp at Judas Farm, near St. Ledger, which had been the scene of much bitter fighting and shelling during the past few days. Consequently there was very little cover of any sort, and bivouacs had to be resorted to and constructed from any material that could be scrounged. Some very rough shelters were made, the great object being to try and make an overhead roof to keep out the rain, which was persistent, the weather having taken a bad turn.

Leaving the farm, we were allotted a position close to the village of Pronville, a mile east of Queant, which had been a strong point in the Hindenburg Line. Geographically the position was almost suicidal. Situated on a road leading out of the village and on a decided incline, our position could not have been more exposed, for our guns were absolutely on the skyline, and must have appeared like a row of haystacks to enemy observers. So nicely up were we that it was possible to see Bourlon Wood, well behind the German lines. Thus somebody was responsible for a really brilliant selection and allocation of position. In spite of the fact of the risk of the position being pointed out to those in authority, we were ordered to carry on.

Naturally we were subjected to much heavy shelling, more so whenever we went into action ourselves. Being more or less under visual observation by the enemy, he seemed to be content as a rule to lie doggo when we were not firing, but once we started he let us have it hot. So we got many thrills and much excitement and, of course, casualties were inevitable, though fortunately not so heavy as might have been expected. Knowledge of the circumstances evidently kept everyone prepared.

Eventually, after a week of this dodging business, it was suddenly appreciated by someone that the position was useless, and with all haste we left and put the guns up a few hundred yards to the rear, where we were in a valley. This naturally meant that our security and safety was perhaps a few degrees better, seeing that we were at least out of sight of the enemy's observers.

This position was in the back gardens of some ruined houses, and some distance from the main Queant road. Some cover from the weather was found in the ruins, and this was much appreciated, as of late we had had no cover at all worthy of the name. Close by was what perhaps had been underground horse lines constructed by the Germans when they were in occupation of the territory. A long ramp led down to a large vault about 15 feet below the surface. The ramp, however, was unprotected, and it was here that a shell fell one day and caught a party of our men, causing much damage and a few casualties, amongst whom were Armourer-Sergeant Stubbs, a good man at his job, and two signallers, Gunners Lloyd and Leake. Being more screened from the enemy we were not interrupted so much and we were in action daily and got through a lot of firing. Ammunition fatigues were more frequent as a consequence, and so once more we began to feel really busy.

After a week of action three guns were moved east of the position, about a mile or so forward to a rather secluded valley just off the Inchy road, but what we gained by seclusion we lost by the utter inaccessibility of the place. The "ammo dump" was quite a route march away, as the lorries were unable to get nearer, and many weary hours were spent, and not a few expletives uttered, when "ammo up" was the order. During one of these fatigues we were unfortunate in losing Capt. Bennett, wounded. Capt. Llewellyn was posted to the Battery a few days later to take his place.

Acting on instructions from Colonel Cotter's Super Heavy Brigade, to which 76 was attached, we lost no time in getting into action. A hold-up of our infantry at the Canal-du-Nord, which was to be crossed, gave us much to do, and we bombarded this spot heavily. With the approach of October the firing was very heavy until this obstacle was overcome, when the bombardment lifted and the infantry went forward. So rapid was their advance that although we had only been here a few days we were surprised to get the order "Cease fire—out of range."

The other three guns were then brought up, and whilst the infantry were making such a strong advance we just hung on and were allowed to stay where we were. During the activities here a German O.K. on a gun detachment, who were putting up a gun, caused many casualties, killed and wounded, Gunner "Lucky" Lucas being amongst those killed (29/9/18). Although we were practically unable to take part in the bombardment we had to stand by for fatigues. One of these was repairing roads up forward, doubtless some of the damage we had done ourselves—an unexpected rod for our back.

After a week of this comparative inactivity we were warned of a visit from Colonel Cotter of the Super Heavies. It caused quite a stir—guns were cleaned up thoroughly and uniforms were as far as possible "poshed" up, boots dubbined and kit collected, and with the search down kitbags a good number of bandoliers were produced and cleaned up, in preparation for the inspection. We were very disappointed, for we got hardly any praise for our appearance and very little in the way of complimentary remarks. The Colonel seemed most alarmed by the fact that our bandoliers were almost all quite empty, and his subsequent remarks were not appreciated. He informed us, however, that we were shortly to go into a new position, and to use his expression, it was a "Hell of a hot shop"— as the infantry had come to a standstill in front of Cambrai! When the parade was over and dismissed, preparations were made for a quick move, but it was found that we could only procure sufficient transport for two guns, and so only two went.

This brought us to October 6th, and so two sub-sections during the late evening left Pronville with the two guns for the position at Noyelles, less than three miles our side of Cambrai, from where we could see the towers and high buildings of the town rising above the horizon, and as the enemy probably used these places as O.P.s it is easily understood why the town was being shelled.

Under cover of darkness the position was reached according to plan, for it had been foreseen that daylight approach would have been folly, especially if any work was to follow. The caution was justified, for although the night passed without harm, many of the Battery will always remember what happened whilst those two gun teams, 40 men, were putting the guns into position early the following morning, October 7th. Firing beams had been laid successfully and the men were starting to mount the guns, when heavy shell fire was directed on them with terrible results. Thirty men of the 40 were casualties, either killed or wounded, the former including Corpl. Hainsworth and Bombr. Lees. Those who could, rendered heroic aid to the wounded, and all deserved the greatest credit for what they did under such awful conditions. Our B.C.A., Fred Abbott, together with Gunner R. Gardner, worked splendidly, and later both were awarded honours in the form of a diploma.

No lines forward having been laid, the rest of the Battery near Pronville were in ignorance of what had happened, and consequently one of those who had escaped unhurt trudged back eight miles to tell them all about it. It was no picnic getting back, and it was a shocked audience that received him and heard his tragic news when he arrived. So the Colonel's remarks about the "Hell of a hot shop" were justified and realized, but it was a terrible blow to us all.

Capt. Llewellyn immediately set off on his motor-cycle to inspect the damage and see for himself exactly what had happened and what work remained yet to be done towards getting both guns ready for action. He found much to be done as only the early stages had been completed, and fortunately the guns were unharmed. During his journey he met Colonel Cotter, to whom he related the events of the morning, and though very sympathetic, the Colonel was emphatic and insisted that the position be carried on with so that those two guns could be ready for action in order to assist in the bombardment, and be manned and gun fire maintained at all costs. Whilst we had men vacancies could be, and had to be, filled. Two more sub-sections were therefore detailed, but the N.C.O.s in charge suggested that only half-sections went, and though it meant harder work, it certainly meant the exposure of less men.

Time was precious, and as soon as possible the men were paraded and despatched in lorries, and were put down at a spot as practicable and safe as possible, proceeding on foot to the position. During the evening, with an hour or two of daylight in hand, the work proceeded, though it was soon apparent that the re-occupation of the position had been observed, for the reception was quite warm, and the work was continually interrupted with dashes for cover. But in spite of this wretched handicap the work went on till midnight, and by that time the two guns were just about ready for action.

This small handful of men had their work fully cut out, for no sooner had they finished with the guns when along came what seemed to them an endless stream of lorries with ammunition, and worst of all, with the position having been occupied so hurriedly, no preparation had been made for receiving it. And so the more crude methods of handling and rolling had to be resorted to, causing the use of much-needed energy, for doubtless it would be needed sooner or later; and sooner it proved to be, for the ammunition was only parked successfully one hour before zero. During these hours of toil the enemy had kept up a very harassing fire, but fortunately not a single casualty occurred in our gallant little party, strange, compared with what happened earlier in the day, but such is fate, some escape and survive over long periods, but with others the baptism of fire is often their only experience.

October 8th broke with an intense bombardment of Cambrai. The firing was indeed severe, and though at first we found ourselves receiving occasional attention from Jerry's long range guns, they soon became silent, and we could only conclude that our advance had been successfully made, and so rapidly perhaps as to cause the enemy to pull his guns out and move. Our conclusions were justified, for later in the day we again received the "Cease fire, out of range" order. This gave ample proof of the extent of the progress made by our infantry and mobile artillery, and the news was indeed very cheering.

Very few in the Battery thought that our stay in this new position would be so short, but nevertheless it was our only action, but at what a cost! Considering the small number of men who went three, and the short time spent there, our casualties were most tragically heavy, comparatively the heaviest at any time.

The Pronville position was kept going as billets for a few days, and as there was no need for the Battery to fire, we were allowed a welcome respite and rest, only fatigues being in orders. The Battery was gathered together and assembled as one at the Noyelles position, and whilst clearing up at Pronville, Corpl. Mann met with a nasty accident. All refuse and rubbish was being collected and burnt, and unfortunately a live rifle bullet got gathered in and exploded on the fire, with the result that a piece of the casing entered Mann's forehead, wounding him so severely that he was sent to hospital.

At Noyelles all guns were dismounted and made ready for the road, in case there should come an emergency call. Everybody then settled down for a few days' relaxation : football matches, pontoon and solo, etc., were enjoyed, and not a few explored the locality and the village.

On October 13th the Battery moved off again to Pronville, an outer suburb of Cambrai, and here our billets afforded us some luxury, for we were all allotted space in houses, in some of which there was even a piano. This accommodation was very much appreciated after the recent exposure we had endured for so long. The Battery was fortunate in having a fairly long stay here as much benefit was gained by the rest, and everyone became more cheerful.

Sandwiched between excursions back to Noyelles on fatigue duty, removing the inevitable ammunition up to our present position, many football matches were arranged and played. Visits were made to Cambrai and to the cinema, which had quickly been got ship-shape and into running order. We began to appreciate that civilization was still in existence, and whilst the chance was offered we made the most of it. But just when we were beginning to like ourselves in this cushy billet the Battery had to leave, after a stay of about three weeks, and again we moved for a rest at Avesnes-les-Aubert, about eight miles in front of Cambrai.

On arrival here, we found that the village was partly in occupation by French civilians who had, until the recent Allied advance, been under the control and discipline of the enemy. Our billets in decent houses were, generally speaking, quite comfortable, and we settled down again to enjoy our new-found happiness and rest from action, as so far as we knew the advance had gone so far ahead that our services were not required.

Fatigues were about the only duties which gave any cause for parades, and once these were done football and walking from place to place were enjoyed by all who wished. Route marches were enjoyed, rifle drill (a bit delayed?) not so much enjoyed, and the Battery orders seemed to be arranged so as to avoid any feeling of laziness or slackness getting a hold on the men.

Except for some German bombing planes, which passed over our billets at night, there was nothing to show during our stay that the war was still going on.

This calm lasted for about two weeks, and so cut off from the rest of the world were we that the great day, November 11th, arrived without our knowing of the important negotiations which had been going on and what the day really meant. In fact, we were all in ignorance of the Armistice having been signed until well after mid-day when a dispatch rider arrived from Brigade H.Q. with the news.

The emotions displayed when the news was made known were far removed from what might well have been expected. One would have thought that all would have gone "up in the air," but though inwardly the relief was profound, no great excitement was shown. Maybe this was largely due to the fact that during the rest we had become accustomed to the quietness and inactivity, and our minds had become settled and content.

And so passed Armistice Day, for which thanks be to God and all who contrived to make it a landmark in history.

During the two weeks that followed the routine was much the same, but the news got round that we were to have new guns. Strange so soon after the Armistice, though those we had had done well, and perhaps could not be wholly depended on for any further accurate shooting if it should be required. By now a railway-track had been laid, following the advance, and at St. Aubert, two miles forward, convenience was found for unloading the new guns.

Everyone was pleased to find that they were Mark IIs, of which we had experience when we took over the guns of 191 Siege Battery in front of Ypres, and found them to be far superior to the Mark I. Though we knew we should never use them, yet it gave us a happy feeling to have the more modern type. A sad farewell was accorded the old Mark Is as they were sent away to Cambrai—to be returned to Ordnance Officer at Calais—and all were sorry to part with such faithful servants, which though old and worn had done extremely well, like the men who had manned them.

Battery orders were more regular now, the new guns were cleaned, and gun drill instituted for the benefit of the reinforcements who had recently arrived to make up strength.

Avesnes-les-Aubert eventually proved to be the final stage in the advance, and on November 27th we turned our backs once more to the line, this time under far less harassing conditions than eight months previously, when everything was confusion and haste. The first trek was for only a short distance back into Cambrai, where the old French Cavalry Barracks were used for our billets, and although lofty and rather cold, they were comfortable. We only remained here for one week, however, during which only fatigue duties and gun cleaning formed the routine.

With the arrival of December we had to pack up our guns, which we had never used. At the railway station the loading was quite a simple matter, as the transporting trucks were those that had been used for bringing up tanks and were exceedingly suitable for the job in hand. Our tractors simply drove straight off the loading stage right on to the truck, towing the gun piece behind—a much easier method than the old way used at Boulogne.

This little task took place about December 2nd or 3rd, and during the evening of the day with everything and everybody aboard the journey commenced : the same old type of transport-de-luxe—"Hommes 40, Chevaux 10." Where we were going to no one seemed to know, but our journey was of the usual type, slow but sure and with many stops, most of which seemed to be needless and unofficial. Eventually the train drew into a siding at Mondicourt, about seven miles from Doullens, and here we were instructed to detrain and unload the guns in the same easy manner in which we loaded them.

Having detrained, we made ready for a road journey and set off towards Doullens, but as we reached the outskirts of the town a turn was taken to the left and another two miles' journey brought us to Authieulle, which proved to be our settled destination. Temporary billets were allotted to us in barns and lofts, and we began to construct a camp of Nissen huts. There were drawn from the field store depôt, and the work was soon in full swing, and shortly before Christmas the camp was ready. We were very happy and comfortable, and with the exception of cook-houses and other outbuildings, for which material had not been provided, all were well housed. Material for the cook-houses had to be secured, and the "usual method" was resorted to : lorries even went as far away as Albert, returning with corrugated iron sheets, pit props, "elephant" irons and odds and ends to complete the equipment of these buildings. Apart from the fatigues arranged, some of which were to assist the Heavy Batteries of the Brigade (who had their horses to consider), our time was leisurely and easy.

Christmas Day arrived, and was spent in a manner which had not been possible during the past two years, and generally speaking, we made the most of the new-found conditions and had a jolly good time.

Major Ramsdale spent much time and trouble in forming a Concert Party called the "Nine-Twos." With the assistance of Lieut. Livesey and a number of other helpers, those who took part were trained, and scenery painted. All who could help did so, and the show developed into quite a successful affair, and proved an asset not only to the Battery, but to those in the vicinity of the village. So successful was the Party that concerts were arranged and given in Doullens, which says much for the talent of the performers and producers, drawn solely from 76.

Amiens and Doullens were well within reach of us all, and many were the trips made to these places. When parades were over, it became the usual thing to visit one or the other and make up for lost time and the good times which had been missed during the past years.

With the arrival of the New Year, preliminary demobilization commenced, and our strength was slowly thinned as various little batches went away home to Blighty, until there remained only a skeleton Battery to take care of the guns and to escort them safely over to England. This event took place during May, guns and stores being transported to the docks at Le Havre. Sergt. Fred Abbott and a small party were left to see them loaded on board a transport, and he was given a fatigue party of 30 Chinese in charge of a Chinese sergeant. And what a motley crew, dressed in all sorts of attire, silk hats and evening dress included. But they knew how to "dodge the column" all right—for it took our chaps almost as much time in chasing them round as it did to load the stores. A small party went with the guns and stores to

Southampton, and the rest of the party returned to England by troopship.

The guns were finally handed over on the Isle of Wight by Major Ramsdale and a small party of N.C.O.s and men, amongst whom were about six members of the original 76 Siege Battery, who had the privilege of being present at the final stage, the winding-up of the Battery of which they and all those others who survived were justly proud, a Battery which carried out its task in an excellent manner.

So ends this chronicle.

EPILOGUE

The foregoing is as near as possible a true record of what 76 Siege Battery did during the Great War. As a fighting unit it certainly carried out the programmes allotted throughout its existence in France with great credit. No unit could have wished for a better body of officers and men than that which from time to time composed its strength.

The four commanding officers were, with the assistance of their junior and section officers, responsible for not only very good work in the field, but also for creating a good sense of comradeship and unity throughout the Battery. All were greatly admired and respected by the N.C.O.s and men, who had implicit trust and faith in them.

Of the N.C.O.s and men, they did their bit—many a grumble, the soldier's privilege, but for all that, stout-hearted, willing and well-disciplined.

Drawn from the Regular, Territorial and Kitchener's Armies, and having had, at the time the Battery was formed, served either in France, on coast defence, anti-aircraft batteries, or as recruits under Lord Derby's scheme, one cannot speak too highly of the excellent way in which these men blended together, from the moment they all met at Horsham. One never need look far for a pal, for there was always one to be found in 76.

From the blending together of such a body of men, in good times and in bad times, there grew a great spirit of good fellowship. Those who survive will cherish and foster that spirit throughout the days to come, and always remember their comrades who fell in the field of Flanders.

ANECDOTES

At Doullens, April, 1936, on the occasion of a parade, Bombr. Jack Fisher scrambled along at the last minute and fell-in with his section minus his putties. Wearing riding breeches he had a pronounced horsey appearance, which elicited the following remark from Sergt.-Major Chinnery : "Where's yer putties, Bombardier? What d'yer think you are, a bleeting jockey?"

* * *

Scene : Night-time at the Friezenberg Ridge position, and the guns in action.

Enemy planes could be heard approaching, and the cease fire was given, as it was feared they were passing overhead.

A Corporal in charge of one of the guns became somewhat irritated by the general tittering and laughter of his gun team. After ordering silence some few times, he at last shouted excitedly : "Shut up, you —— fools, they'll 'ear yer."

* * *

Who was the poor gunner who lost a map on his way to the O.P. and was made to go to the O.P. three consecutive mornings to try and find it, and then got seven days' pay, all because the Sergeants codded Sergt.-Major Chinnery that the Sergeants' Mess was clearly marked on the aforesaid map?

* * *

" One on the Colonel."

When at Brielen Road, Ypres, ammunition had been unloaded during the night and safely stowed away. Behind a hedge to the left rear of us, an 8 inch battery, which also had had a load of ammunition up at the same time.

When our lot was put away, everyone retired to their dug-outs in the back garden. Just as day was breaking

99

we were all rudely awakened by a rasping voice shouting through the gas blanket: "Who's in charge here?", the owner of the voice being the Group Colonel, who was on an early surprise visit.

A bombardier who was in charge suddenly awoke, and being fully dressed jumped up, squeezed through the door, saluted and said, "I am, sir!", at which the Colonel looked him up and down, assuming an expression of understanding. The following dialogue took place.

Col. : "Had any ammunition to-night, Bombardier?"

Bombr. : "Yes, sir."

Col. : "Then why didn't you have the charges put away in their proper places?"

Bombr. : "I did, sir!"

Col. : "I say you did not!"

Bombr. : "Pardon me, sir, I did!"

Col. : "Come with me, then, and I'll show you that you did not."

Both walked round to unloading point beside ruined house, and there neatly stacked up against the wall was quite a lot of drums, which to the experienced eye obviously contained 8 inch cartridges. Pointing to these the Colonel exclaimed : "There you are, now contradict me if you dare."

Bombr. : "With pleasure, sir; we do not make it a rule to fire our 9.2 guns with 8 inch charges."

The Colonel, realizing his mistake, partially collapsed, but without any apology retreated silently to the 8 inch battery, there to vent his wrath on some unfortunate soul, and to get even with someone for the embarrassment he suffered at 76. Shortly after, the stack of drums had disappeared, so doubtless the Colonel enjoyed his breakfast.

* * *

Thelus will be remembered by some who recall a slip by a section officer on duty during firing who was advised from the O.P. to order one gun 25 degrees more right. The gun had already 50 degrees right, and he shouted—"Gun, Seven, five minutes right!"

Of how Mr. Showan needing a leather jerkin on account of the cold, mentioned the fact to Jock Clelland, who, like the duteous servant he was, secured one for him by the early hours of the next day. How pleased and thankful was Mr. Showan as he walked into the mess for breakfast—but what did Steve think about it ?

* * *

How religiously we marched at night round Harwich on "tip toes" practising for artillery on the move on active service. How we slopped and ground our feet into the mud when we actually got to France, caring little for noise with gun fire everywhere. "Tip toes !" Bah !

* * *

How many will recall with amusement and admiration the incident when Wheeler Gunner Jimmy Sawer stopped a number of flying splinters from an H.E. shell, and his cool remark : "I feel like a pepper-pot, covered with holes all over." So typical of Jimmy.

* * *

One about "Ammo" told by the B.C.A.

It was on the occasion of moving up from Cambridge Road to Frezenburg Ridge, the Colonel had suddenly asked how many lorries we should require to move the shells. Our return showed three hundred rounds, so I told the Major there were probably more, as when ammunition arrived during the night it was impossible to check it. I had tried to keep on the right side to prevent a shortage in case of a sudden order to "strafe," and so I felt sure that there were well over three hundred.

"All right," said the Major, "we'll order a couple of extra lorries. If there are any left we can dump them." As a matter of fact, we found it necessary to dump about a thousand !

I often wonder what those poor gunners, who had rolled them about in the mud, losing sleep and suffering inconvenience, would have done to me had they known who was responsible.

ROLL OF HONOUR

Major O. WAKEFORD, M.C.	- Killed in Action	21/3/18
Captain G. L. ANDREWS -	- ,, ,,	3/5/18
Lieutenant R. W. SATCHWELL -	,, ,,	31/1/17
Gunner ALSTON, L. - -	- ,, ,,	5/9/17
,, ASHURST, A. H. -	- Died of Wounds	5/11/17
,, BUCKOKE, W. -	- Killed in Action	24/9/17
,, BURTON, A. - -	- ,, ,,	4/11/17
,, BROWN, T. - -	- ,, ,, .	10/12/17
,, BRACKLEY, H. -	- ,, ,,	24/3/18
,, BAILEY, J. T. -	- ,, ,,	7/10/18
,, BENSON, H. - -	- ,, ,,	24/7/17
,, CLELLAND, R. -	- ,, ,,	4/7/17
,, COPE, H. W. -	- ,, ,,	14/10/17
,, CRAMPIN, A. J. -	- ,, ,,	13/12/17
,, CRUISE, W. E. -	- ,, ,,	26/3/18
,, COWARD, E. -	- ,, ,,	7/10/18
,, COOPER, G. - -	- ,, ,,	24/6/17
,, CONQUEST, W. -	- ,, ,,	24/7/17
,, DIXON, A. - -	- ,, ,,	24/6/17
,, DAVIES, R. - -	- ,, ,,	23/3/18
,, EDMANDS, A. E. -	- ,, ,,	1/10/17
,, GABRIEL, S. A. -	- ,, ,,	21/8/17
,, GOLDSMITH, E. -	- ,, ,,	7/10/18
Corporal HAINSWORTH, T. -	- ,, ,,	7/10/18
Gunner HARLEY, C. - -	- Died of Wounds	10/7/17
,, HUTTON, H. E. -	- Killed in Action	21/3/18
,, HUNT, B. - -	- ,, ,,	30/6/17
,, INGHAM, C. - -	- ,, ,,	7/10/18
,, JONES, H. W. -	- Died of Wounds	15/7/17
,, JONES, T. - -	- Killed in Action	4/11/17
,, KINGSLEY, S. C. -	- ,, ,,	24/7/17
,, LEAKE, J. H. -	- ,, ,,	21/9/18

Gunner	LLOYD, F. J. - -	,,	,,	20/9/18
,,	LESTER, S. - - -	,,	,,	7/10/18
,,	LEES, D. - - -	,,	,,	7/10/18
,,	LUCAS, T. - - -	,,	,,	8/10/18
,,	McCULLOCH, A. - -	,,	,,	7/10/18
,,	MILLER, F. - - -	,,	,,	6/11/17
,,	MORRIS, E. - -	Died of Wounds		1/5/17
,,	ORMEROD, F. - -	Killed in Action		4/11/17
,,	OSMAN, R. E. - -	,,	,,	22/5/18
,,	OLDFIELD, W. - -	,,	,,	14/10/18
,,	PENNEY, J. - - -	,,	,,	10/12/17
,,	PETTIFER, S. C. - -	,,	,,	7/10/18
,,	PATERNOSTER, A. - -	,,	,,	4/11/17
,,	POYER, S. C. - -	Died of Wounds		7/11/17
A./Cpl.	RAEBURN, A. E. - -	,,	,,	27/7/17
Gunner	STEPHENSON, H. S. -	Killed in Action		24/9/17
,,	TATE, P. A. - - -	,,	,,	10/12/17
,,	WALKER, W. - -	,,	,,	22/5/18
,,	WINTER, A. J. - -	,,	,,	7/10/18
,,	WELCH, S. B. - -	,,	,,	24/7/17
,,	WAKEFIELD, L. - -	,,	,,	27/7/17
,,	UPHAM, E. J. - -	Died of Wounds		10/7/17
,,	JORDAN, F. - - -	Killed in Action.		Date unknown.
,,	LEWIS, E. - - -	Killed in Action		after leaving 76.

AWARDS

Major F. A. W. Cobbold - Distinguished Service Order.

Major E. N. Aston - - Military Cross.

Major O. Wakeford - - Military Cross.

Major A. Sandercock - - Member of the British Empire.

Captain F. H. Ashworth - Order of St. Anna (2nd Class). Mentioned in Despatches.

2nd Lieutenant P. Grange - Military Cross.

2nd Lieutenant H. J. Johnston Military Cross.

2nd Lieutenant H. A. Rist - Belgian Croix du Guerre.

Sergeant J. Semple - - Distinguished Conduct Medal (King's Birthday Honours).

Sergeant E. Wilks - - Military Medal.

Sergeant A. E. Mudge - - Military Medal (Conspicuous Bravery under Shell Fire).

Corporal D. Rose - - - Military Medal.

Bombardier A. Bentall - Military Medal (Gallantry and Devotion to Duty under Shell Fire).

Gunner N. Quigley - - Military Medal (Gallantry and Devotion to Duty under Shell Fire).

Gunner S. Cooper - - Military Medal.

Gunner J. Wilson - - - Military Medal.

Bombardier H. W. Fenner - Military Medal.

Sergeant F. Abbott - - Diploma.

Corporal R. Gardner - - Diploma.

Sergeant J. A. Watson - - Mentioned in Despatches after leaving 76 Siege Battery.

L./Corporal W. Hallgarth, (M.T.A.S.C.) Military Medal (Devotion to Duty and Gallantry under Shell Fire).

ORIGINAL PERSONNEL OF 76 SIEGE BATTERY R.G.A.

(SUBSEQUENT PROMOTIONS IN BRACKETS)

Major R. H. Brent Clark. To Hospital, 8/9/16.
Capt. F. A. W. Cobbold (Major). To Hospital (wounded), 4/7/17.
Lieut. E. N. Aston (Major). Transferred, Dec./16.
,, E. Starkey (Captain). To Hospital, Nov./17.
,, F. H. Ashworth (Captain). To Hospital (wounded), 9/7/16.
,, A. Sandercock (Major). To Hospital (shell shock), 29/7/16.

REGULARS AND KITCHENER'S ARMY.

Bombr. Arnold (Cpl.). To Hospital, 5/12/17.
,, Baker, T. To Hospital (sick), 13/9/17. Invalided to England, 24/9/17.
Gnr. Congrave, A. To Hospital (sick), 26/10/17.
,, Clarke, G. To Hospital (wounded), 24/7/17. Invalided to England, 3/8/17.
,, Clelland, R. Killed in action, 4/7/17.
B.S.M. Chinnery, W. To England for discharge, 13/12/16. Later seen in Cambrai.
Gnr. Drake, W. F. Demobilized.
,, Duxfield, A. W. To Hospital (wounded), 21/8/17. Invalided to England, 26/8/17.
,, Francis, S. To Hospital (sick), 4/4/16.
,, Frisby, A. To Hospital (sick), 8/10/17.
,, Freeman, F. H. To Hospital (wounded), 3/5/18. Invalided to England, 11/6/18.
,, Glue, W. H. To Hospital (wounded), 16/2/17.
,, Gale, P. To Hospital (whilst on leave to U.K.).
,, Gooch, F. To England, 3/10/16, for Cadet's Course.
,, Hodges, R. E. (Bombr.). Demobilized.
,, Hutchins, A. To Hospital (sick), 30/10/18.
,, Harris, T. (A/Bombr.). Invalided to England (sick), 3/10/16.
,, Jones, T. (L/Bombr.). Demobilized.
,, Liston, E. To Hospital (gassed), 2/11/17. Invalided to England, 7/11/17.
,, Lees, D. (Bdr.). Killed in action, 6/10/18.
,, Lucas, F. Died, 8/10/18, of wounds received in action, 6/10/18.
,, Murray, J. P. (Cpl.). Demobilized, 26/1/19.
,, McAuliffe, J. Invalided to England (sick), 15/5/17.

Gnr.	Mayfield, J. (Bombr.). Transferred to Home Estab., 7/1/19.
,,	Marsh, R. A. To Hospital (sick), 14/3/17.
,,	Marchbanks, W. To Hospital (wounded), 24/8/16. Invalided to England, 5/9/16.
,,	Melvin, W. To Hospital (sick), 11/9/16.
Cpl.	Mudge, A. E. (Sergt.). Promoted to B.Q.M.S. and posted to 443 S. Bty., 7/10/18.
Gnr.	Molesworth, W. (Ftr./Cpl.). To Hospital (gassed), 15/7/17. Invalided to England, 5/8/17.
B.Q.M.S.	Moore, T. J. Posted to 5th Army Arty. School as instr., 12/11/16.
Bombr.	Mitton, W. (Cpl.). To Hospital (sick), 25/10/17.
Gnr.	Maguire, D. (Bombr.). To England, 28/7/16, for release for munition work.
Cpl.	Nunn, A. W. (Sergt.). To Home Estab., 8/2/19.
Gnr.	Norgate, W. To Hospital (sick), 21/4/16.
Sergt.	Oliver, R. To Home Estab., 19/3/17.
,,	Potter, G. Promoted B.Q.M.S., and posted to 56 S. Bty. R.G.A., 9/11/16.
Cpl.	Percival, J. (Sergt.). Invalided to England (crushed hand), 1/7/17.
Gnr.	Paternoster, A. Killed in action, 4/11/17.
,,	Perrin, G. W. Transferred to R.E., 24/2/17.
,,	Parminter, F. To Hospital (sick), 5/11/16. Invalided to England, 18/11/16.
,,	Puig, W. To Hospital (sick), 15/8/17.
,,	Quigley, N. Re-engaged for 21 years. Posted to England, 14/3/17.
Cpl.	Ridge, P. (Sergt.). To England, 21/1/17, for Cadet's Course.
Bombr.	Ridley, G. Marked P.B. and sent to Base, 1/12/16.
,,	Robbins. To Hospital (sick), 19/1/17. Invalided to England, 31/1/17.
Gnr.	Robbins, J. To Hospital (sick), 31/10/17. Invalided to England, 13/11/17.
,,	Roberts, W. To Hospital (gassed), 23/7/17.
,,	Roberts, J. To Hospital (heat stroke), 5/6/17. Invalided to England, 9/6/17.
,,	Ramshawe, H. To Hospital (injured), 1/11/18.
Ftr./Cpl.	Raeburn, D. A. Killed in action, 24/7/17.
Gnr.	Salvidge, A. To Hospital (sick), 9/2/17. Invalided to England, 23/10/17.
Bombr.	Semple, W. (Sergt.). To Home Estab.
Gnr.	Simons, T. (Bombr.). To Hospital (sick), 7/11/17. Invalided to England, 13/11/17.

Gnr.   Thyer, T. To Hospital (sick), 14/9/16.

,,   Turner, A. M. To Hospital (sick), 7/11/17.

,,   Whitehead, H. (Bombr.). To Hospital (injured), 11/5/18. Invalided to England, 21/5/18.

,,   Whiteside, H. To Hospital (wounded), 24/7/17. Invalided to England, 30/7/17.

Cpl.   Watson, J. A. (Sergt.). To England, 17/2/17, for Cadet's Course.

Bombr.   Western, A. E. (Cpl.). To Hospital (wounded), 20/6/17. Invalided to England, 28/6/17.

,,   Wilks, W. E. (Sergt.). Demobilized.

Gnr.   Whalley, J. To Hospital (gassed), 23/7/17. Invalided to England, 12/8/18.

,,   Waugh, J. To Hospital (wounded), 9/7/17. Invalided to England, 16/7/17.

Cpl.   Wringe, W. J. To Hospital (shell shock), 19/8/16. Invalided to England, 23/8/16.

,,   Willis, H. E. (Sergt.). To Hospital (sick), 21/11/17. Invalided to England, 26/11/17.

Gnr.   Walker, J. Demobilized.

Sergt.   Williams, F. Promoted B.Q.M.S., and posted to 46 S. Bty. R.G.A., 2/11/16.

TERRITORIALS.

Gnr.   Abbott, F. C. (Sergt.). Still with Unit.

,,   Baker, G. (Bombr.). Still with Unit.

,,   Barton, A. To Hospital (wounded), 21/3/18. To England, 25/3/18.

,,   Bennet, A. To Hospital (sick), 25/11/16. Eventually discharged.

Bombr.   Bentall, A. (Cpl.). To England, 24/2/18, for Cadet's Course.

Gnr.   Bigsby, J. To Hospital (wounded), 7/10/18. To England, 11/10/18.

Bombr.   Blowers, W. To Ordnance Workshop and eventually transferred.

Gnr.   Bowling, H. To Hospital (sick), 2/5/18.

,,   Brown, C. A. To Hospital (wounded), 22/4/18. To England, 19/5/18.

,,   Buckoke, W. Killed in action, 24/9/17.

,,   Bultitude, G. (Cpl.). Still with Unit.

,,   Butcher, S. To Hospital (injured), 27/3/18.

,,   Chapman, W. To Hospital (wounded), 24/6/17. To England, 18/7/17.

,,   Conquest, W. Killed in action, 24/7/17.

,,   Cook, L. To Hospital (sick), 12/11/17.

Gnr.	Coote, W. To Hospital (wounded), 7/4/17. To England, 10/4/17.
Cpl.	Cornell, F. (Sergt.). To Hospital (shell shock), 2/6/17.
Gnr.	Cox, R. A. Demobilized, 25/1/19.
,,	Cracknell, A. To Hospital, 13/1/17. To England, 22/1/17.
,,	Cuff, H. (L./Bombr.). Still with Unit.
,,	Curry, F. M. To Hospital (sick).
,,	Cutting, F. (Bombr.). To Hospital (injured), 24/3/18. To England, 29/3/18.
,,	Day, D. W. To Hospital (sick), 5/12/16.
,,	Drake, G. (Cpl.). To Hospital (sick), 11/11/17.
,,	Durrant, F. To Hospital (wounded), 17/9/17. To England, 21/9/17.
Bombr.	Fenner, H. (Cpl.). To Hospital (wounded), 24/6/17.
Gnr.	Fidgett, H. W. To Hospital (gassed), 23/7/17.
,,	Fisher, J. (Bombr.). To Hospital (wounded), 15/7/17. To England, 3/8/17.
,,	Freeman, H. To Hospital (gassed), 2/11/17. To England, 15/11/17.
,,	Gaches, A. Transferred to R.E., 16/4/17.
,,	Gardner, R. (Cpl.). Still with Unit.
,,	Gibbard, J. (Bombr.). To Hospital (wounded), 24/9/17. To England, 7/10/17.
,,	Gibbard, B. To Hospital (sick), whilst on leave to U.K.
Bombr.	Grundy, J. (Cpl.). To England, 8/2/17, for Cadet's Course.
Gnr.	Hainsworth, T. (Cpl.). Killed in action, 7/10/18.
,,	Hills, R. To Hospital (sick), 12/8/16. To England, 21/8/16.
,,	Hockley, W. (Cpl.). Still with Unit.
,,	Hoffman, A. To Hospital (wounded), 2/6/17. To England, 8/6/17.
,,	How, H. Demobilized, 22/1/19.
,,	Jordan, F. To Hospital (sick), 27/2/18, whilst on leave to U.K.
,,	Kirkman, J. To Hospital (sick), 20/1/17. To England, 29/1/17.
,,	Kitson, A. To Hospital (sick), 28/7/16. To England, 15/8/16.
,,	Lambert, J. R. To Hospital (sick), 1/6/18. To England, 10/6/18.
,,	Lee, C. A. (Bombr.). Demobilized, 13/12/18.
,,	Lewis, P. To Hospital, 12/4/17.
,,	Ling, S. Transferred to R.E., 25/4/17.

Gnr.	Lock, W. (Serg.). Still with Unit.
,,	Last, R. (Cpl.). Demobilized.
,,	Looker, S. To Hospital (injured), 27/2/18. To England, 30/9/18.
,,	Laughlin, B. To Hospital (injured), 10/2/18. To England, 7/3/18.
Bombr.	Mallows, G. O. (Cpl.). To England, 19/12/16, for Cadet's Course.
Gnr.	Mann, R. To Hospital (sick), 6/8/17.
,,	Martin, H. To Hospital (wounded), 2/9/17.
,,	Meekins, C. To Hospital (wounded), 10/7/17.
,,	Newson, G. To Hospital (wounded), 24/7/17. To England, 10/8/17.
,,	Palmer, H. To England, 4/2/17, for Cadet's Course.
,,	Papworth, J. (Sergt.). Demobilized, 6/2/19.
,,	Penney, J. Killed in action, 10/12/17.
,,	Penstone, L. To England (gassed), 4/8/17.
,,	Peach, S. To Hospital (wounded), 22/5/18. To England, 9/6/18.
B.Q.M.S.	Potter, A. E. With Army of the Rhine (volunteer).
Cpl.	Robinson, K. A. To England, 15/10/16, for Cadet's Course.
Gnr.	Rose, D. E. (Cpl.). To England, 27/8/17, for Cadet's Course.
Bombr.	Rumsey, L. To England (wounded), 11/11/17.
,,	Runacles, B. To Hospital (wounded), 17/9/17. To England, 21/9/17.
W./Gnr.	Sawer, J. To Hospital (wounded), 29/6/17.
Bombr.	Shee, E. N. (Cpl.). To England, 12/2/17, for Cadet's Course.
Gnr.	Slade, P. To Hospital (sick), 31/8/17. To England, 4/9/17.
,,	Smith, G. W. Demobilized, 3/2/19.
,,	Smith, C. To England (gassed), 5/11/17.
Sergt.	Streeter, F. Promoter to B.Q.M.S., and posted to 27th S. Bty., 4/1/17.
Gnr.	Sullivan, H. To Hospital (shell shock), 5/6/17.
,,	Thomas, H. Still with Unit.
,,	Thurston, J. (Sgt.). Still with Unit.
,,	Tucker, G. To Hospital (sick), 23/6/17.
,,	Walford, F. (Bombr.). To Hospital (sick), 13/9/18. To England, 2/10/18.
,,	Watts, A. To England (sick), 1/11/17.
,,	Westley, E. To Hospital (wounded), 22/5/18.
,,	Wright, O. To England (sick), 9/6/17. (Aged 17 years, after two years' service with the Battery.)

MEMBERS OF 76 SIEGE BATTERY AND COLUMN OLD COMRADES' ASSOCIATION.

Major E. N. Aston, c/o Lloyds Bank, Pall Mall, S.W.

S. Arnold, 135 Watling Avenue, Burnt Oak, Edgware, Middlesex.

F. Abbott, Holly Cottage (next P.O.), Holbrook, Ipswich.

Capt. F. H. Ashworth, Whitestones, Chapel eu le Frith, Derbyshire.

T. Baker, 110 College Place, Camden Town, N.W.

Q.M.S. Byron (R.A.O.C.), 49 Appledore Avenue, Barnhurst, Kent.

O. Ball, 11 Hadleigh Road, Ipswich.

A. Bentall, Little Wakering, Great Wakering, Essex.

J. Brown, The Forge, High Street, Great Wakering, Essex.

G. Baker, The Bucks Head, Thwaites, St. George, Eye.

G. Bultitude, Pin Mill Road, Chelmondiston, Ipswich.

G. Butcher, 41 Cavendish Street, Ipswich (or c/o Union Hotel).

L. Barnes, Ebor, Kellett Road, Southampton.

C. A. Browne, "Shirley," Ambleside Drive, Southend-on-Sea.

J. Bigsby, 37 Crowstone Road, Little Thurrock, Grays, Essex.

Y. C. Boorman, 6 Sutherland Place, Bayswater, W.3.

Major F. A. W. Cobbold, D.S.O., Church Close, Sproughton, Ipswich.

A. J. Cracknell, 75a Princess May Road, Stoke Newington, N.16.

J. Cuff, 49 Salisbury Road, Ipswich.

F. Cutting, 6 St. David's Road, Ipswich.

G. Curry, Hawthorne, Lancaster Avenue, Hitchin, Herts.

G. Cox, Fletchwood, Ernest Road, Hornchurch, Essex.

Major R. H. Brent Clark, Albion Chambers, Bristol.

R. A. Cox, 85 Windsor Road, Ilford, Essex.

W. Coote, 12 Tennyson Avenue, Southend-on-Sea.

D. W. Day, Belvedere, Warwick Road, Rayleigh, Essex.

G. Drake, 14 Rands Way, Ipswich.

A. Duxfield, Grascroft Cottage, Chester Road, Grappenhall, Cheshire.

A. F. Drake, 438 Whitehall Road, Bristol.

F. Durrant, Market Hill, Framlingham, Suffolk.

J. E. Fisher, 7 Rhodesia Road, Leytonstone, E.11.

H. Freeman, 84 Southview Drive, Westcliff-on-Sea.

A. E. Gaches, 9 Maudesley Road, Well Hall, Eltham, S.E.9.

W. Godwin, 167 Church Road, Manor Park, E.12.

Capt. S. Godlee, Denehurst, Barnt Green, Birmingham.

E. Gunton, 23 London Road, Chatteris, Cambs.

F. Gooch, 8 Tulketh Street, Southport, Lancs.

J. W. Grundy, Research Station, Harpur Hill, Buxton, Derby.

H. How, 26 Preston Road, Leytonstone, E.11.
R. Hodges, Park Wall, Holly Grove, Northenden Road, Sale, Cheshire.
A. Hoffman, 42 High Dene, Walsworth, Hitchin, Herts.
A. Hutchins, 33 Aylett Road, South Norwood, S.E.25.
C. A. Lee, Church End, Foulness Island, Essex.
R. J. Last, 2 Brooklyn Villas, Wetherden, Stowmarket, Suffolk.
H. Laughlin, Victoria Street, Ipswich.
W. H. Lowry, 4 Osterley Avenue, Isleworth, Middlesex.
W. Lock, 1 North End, St. Denys, Southampton.
J. P. Murray, 6 Cotham Gardens, Redland, Bristol.
C. Meekins, Wilford Cottages, near Bromeswell, Woodbridge.
G. O. Mallows, 6 Tufnell House, 73 Anson Road, Tufnell Park, N.W.5.
S./M. A. Martin, 225 Gladstone Street, Peterborough.
H. Newbold, Ivydene, 27 Mercers Road, Holloway, N.7.
G. Newson, 73 Gainsborough Road, Felixstowe.
R. Oliver, 25 Bayham Street, Camden Town, N.W.1.
H. E. Palmer, 57 Stanthorpe Road, Streatham, S.W.16.
J. Papworth, 68 Sheaveshill Avenue, Colindale, N.W.9.
T. S. Peach, Railway Cottages, Marks Tey, near Colchester.
A. Potter, 79 Vernon Street, Ipswich.
J. Percival, 105 Northcote Avenue, Southall, Middlesex.
B. Runnacles, 13 Church Road, Felixstowe.
W. Rook, 10 Barnett Road, Brighton.
L. Rumsey, Scotts Field Cottage, Copdock, Ipswich.
D. Rose, M.M., Station House, Ruckholt Road, Leyton.
J. Sawer, 4 Constable Road, Felixstowe.
C. Smith, Council Terrace, St. Andrews Road, Felixstowe.
E. Shee, 39 Dudley Road, Ilford, Essex.
J. A. Sampson, 7 Redington Road, Hampstead, N.W.3.
D. Scott, Duck Street, Brettenham, Suffolk.
T. Stone, 1 Moors Avenue, South Stafford, Grays, Essex.
W. Semple, D.C.M., Watleys End, Winterbourne, near Bristol.
P. B. Showan, 11 Parkhill Road, Hampstead, N.W.3.
A. Sivyer, 6 Kingston Road, Merton, Surrey.
H. Sullivan, 22 Munster Way, Hornchurch, Essex.
R. G. Smith, 126 Sixth Avenue, Manor Park, E.12.
Major A. Sandercock, c/o Trengrouse Nathan Ltd., 51/55 Tooley Street, S.E.1. Charlwood Park Farm, Horley, Surrey.
F. Streeter, 24 Belle Vue Road, Southend-on-Sea.
Capt. E. Starkey, 59 Tyrwhitt Road, Lewisham High Street, St. John's, S.E.1.
B. Thurston, 144 High Street, Felixstowe.
M. Turner, "Vermelles," 35 Etwall Road, Hall Green, Birmingham.

H. Thomas, 69 Chesterton Road, Plaistow, E.13.
F. Westley, 7 Hythe Road, Wraysbury, Bucks.
F. Walford, 154 Trafalgar Street, Walworth, S.E.17.
D. Watts, 184 Hainault Avenue, Westcliff-on-Sea.
F. Williams, Artillery House, Central Avenue, Southend-on-Sea.
H. E. Willis, The Lodge, Bere Hill, Andover, Hants.
J. A. Watson, Ashton House, Easingwold, Yorks.
C. Whitehead, 28 Williamson Avenue, Peterborough.
O. Wright, 69 Broom Hill Road, Ipswich.
L. F. Penstone (Hon. Sec.), 69 Church Drive, North Harrow, Middlesex.

M.T.A.S.C.

F. J. Ball, 20 Rose Street, Temple, Bristol.
E. W. Fenner, 12 Trant Road, Thornton Heath, Surrey.
J. G. Greenleaf, 26 Myrtle Road, Hounslow, Middlesex.
E. V. L. Hall, 20 Ambrose Avenue, Golders Green, N.W.3.
W. Howarth, Bryn-Teg, Medlock Road, Woodhouses, Ashton-under-Lyne.
W. P. Hallgarth, M.M., 54/56 Lumley Road, Skegness, Lincolnshire.
C. Kelsey, 3 Cross Street, Market Harborough, Leicestershire.
A. Kilbourn, 86 Lancaster Road, West Norwood, S.E.27.
H. Lawrence, 32 Middleton Avenue, Greenford, Middlesex.
T. J. Lee, 15 Ampthill Street, Bedford.
D. Lyle, 11 St. Lukes Avenue, Maidstone.
R. Mynn, 85 Ansdell Road, Peckham, S.E.15.
W. D. Mudie, 49 High Street, Thames Ditton, Surrey.
R. H. Meats, 107 Fosse Road, South Leicester.
J. Mountjoy, 11 Frederick Street, Caledonian Road, N.1.
W. G. Magrath, 75 High Street, Clapham, S.W.4.
J. J. Pratt, Hillcrest, Long Ashton, Bristol.
B. H. Pippard, 38 Playfield Crescent, East Dulwich, S.E.22.
D. Penman, 98 Elfreda Court, Bellingham, Kent.
R. J. Riggs, Anderson, Blandford, Dorset.
L. Selmour, 10 Peel Terrace, Peel Street, Nottingham.
E. S. McK. Stewart, Lexham Mansions Hotel, Lexham Gardens, W.8.
E. H. Wilson, 84 Chenies Mews, Chenies Street, Tottenham Court Road, W.1.